Alfred Hitchcock's *Psycho* and Taxidermy

Alfred Hitchcock's *Psycho* and Taxidermy

Fashioning Corpses

Subarna Mondal

BLOOMSBURY ACADEMIC
NEW YORK • LONDON • OXFORD • NEW DELHI • SYDNEY

BLOOMSBURY ACADEMIC
Bloomsbury Publishing Inc, 1359 Broadway, New York, NY 10018, USA
Bloomsbury Publishing Plc, 50 Bedford Square, London, WC1B 3DP, UK
Bloomsbury Publishing Ireland, 29 Earlsfort Terrace, Dublin 2, D02 AY28, Ireland

BLOOMSBURY, BLOOMSBURY ACADEMIC and the Diana logo are
trademarks of Bloomsbury Publishing Plc

First published in the United States of America 2024
Paperback edition published 2025

Copyright © Subarna Mondal, 2024

For legal purposes the Acknowledgments on p. ix constitute an
extension of this copyright page.

Cover design by Eleanor Rose
Cover image © Arindam Chatterjee
Work from the art collection of Ashima Obhan and Essenese Obhan

All rights reserved. No part of this publication may be: i) reproduced or transmitted in any form, electronic or mechanical, including photocopying, recording or by means of any information storage or retrieval system without prior permission in writing from the publishers; or ii) used or reproduced in any way for the training, development or operation of artificial intelligence (AI) technologies, including generative AI technologies. The rights holders expressly reserve this publication from the text and data mining exception as per Article 4(3) of the Digital Single Market Directive (EU) 2019/790.

Bloomsbury Publishing Inc does not have any control over, or responsibility for, any third-party websites referred to or in this book. All internet addresses given in this book were correct at the time of going to press. The author and publisher regret any inconvenience caused if addresses have changed or sites have ceased to exist, but can accept no responsibility for any such changes.

Library of Congress Cataloging-in-Publication Data
Names: Mondal, Subarna, author.
Title: Alfred Hitchcock's Psycho and taxidermy : fashioning corpses / Subarna Mondal.
Description: New York : Bloomsbury Academic, 2024. | Includes
bibliographical references and index. |
Summary: "An investigation into how Alfred Hitchcock's Psycho (1960) significantly contributes to the Body Horrors of mainstream narrative cinema through the literal and metaphoric use of the cultural practice of Victorian and modern taxidermy"– Provided by publisher.
Identifiers: LCCN 2023032739 (print) | LCCN 2023032740 (ebook) |
ISBN 9798765101186 (hardback) | ISBN 9798765101223 (paperback) |
ISBN 9798765101193 (epub) | ISBN 9798765101209 (pdf) | ISBN 9798765101216
Subjects: LCSH: Psycho (Motion picture : 1960) | Taxidermy in motion pictures.
Classification: LCC PN1997.P79 M66 2024 (print) | LCC PN1997.P79 (ebook) |
DDC 791.43/72–dc23/eng/20230815
LC record available at https://lccn.loc.gov/2023032739
LC ebook record available at https://lccn.loc.gov/2023032740

ISBN:	HB:	979-8-7651-0118-6
	PB:	979-8-7651-0122-3
	ePDF:	979-8-7651-0120-9
	eBook:	979-8-7651-0119-3

Typeset by Integra Software Services Pvt. Ltd.

For product safety related questions contact productsafety@bloomsbury.com.

To find out more about our authors and books visit www.bloomsbury.com
and sign up for our newsletters.

For Debabrata

Contents

List of Figures   viii
Acknowledgments   ix

Introduction—"Live Forever by Dying Today": Taxidermy, Corporeal Gothic, and Alfred Hitchcock's *Psycho*   1

1. Speciesism and Sexism: Norma Bates and Her Victorian Predecessors   19
2. Norma's Home and Norman's Diorama: Taxidermy, Longing, and Nostalgia   41
3. Illusory Souvenirs: Memory, Beauty, and Hitchcock's Women in *Psycho*, *Vertigo*, *The Birds*, and *Marnie*   63
4. Hitchcock's Installation: *Psycho*'s Shower Stabbing, *Frenzy*'s Serial Strangling, and the Beginning of Slashers   85
5. Fellow-Stuffers: Post-*Psycho* Body Horrors   123

Bibliography   143
Index   152

Figures

1.1	Walter Potter's "The Kittens' Wedding" (1890)	25
1.2	Charles Waterton's "Nondescript" (1824)	34
2.1	*Psycho*, dir. Alfred Hitchcock (1960)	60
3.1	*Psycho*, dir. Alfred Hitchcock (1960)	72
3.2	*Marnie*, dir. Alfred Hitchcock (1964)	83
3.3	*The Birds*, dir. Alfred Hitchcock (1963)	83
4.1	*Psycho*, dir. Alfred Hitchcock (1960)	91
4.2	*Frenzy*, dir. Alfred Hitchcock (1972)	108
4.3	*Frenzy*, dir. Alfred Hitchcock (1972)	109
4.4	*Frenzy*, dir. Alfred Hitchcock (1972)	109
4.5	Kate Clark's "Licking the Plate" (2014)	111
4.6	*Frenzy*, dir. Alfred Hitchcock (1972)	112
4.7	*Frenzy*, dir. Alfred Hitchcock (1972)	115
4.8	*Frenzy*, dir. Alfred Hitchcock (1972)	116
4.9	*Frenzy*, dir. Alfred Hitchcock (1972)	116
5.1	*The Skin I Live In*, dir. Pedro Almodóvar (2011)	130
5.2	*The Skin I Live In*, dir. Pedro Almodóvar (2011)	136
5.3	*The Skin I Live In*, dir. Pedro Almodóvar (2011)	136

Acknowledgments

The idea to work on the art of taxidermy and Hitchcock's *Psycho* occurred to me in 2014 when I was in a hospital bed after a road accident with five broken nasal bones and a concussion on my head. This idea became the basis of my thesis and later formed the premise of the present book. Writing a book with the body at its center, I first need to thank my body for repeatedly cooperating with me in a bizarre way and providing me with the much-needed medical leaves that helped me complete this book in time. A fractured ankle followed shortly by a fractured tailbone followed shortly by the removal of gall bladder followed shortly by a second COVID-19 infection made me stay in bed with the luxury of longer reading hours. While my body adjusted to fractures and organ removal, the bodies in my book steadily took shape. The others who played a significant role in the "fashioning" of this book need to be mentioned now.

I express my gratitude to the reviewers who have given me valuable suggestions at crucial stages of the draft of the book. I cannot thank my editor, Katie Gallof, enough for her constant support and her prompt responses to my numerous queries. I thank Alyssa Jordan, my friend Sayan Mandal, and my student Swarnava Chaudhuri for helping me with the images of the book. I am immensely grateful to Kate Clark for not only letting me use her photograph of one of her creations but actually taking the trouble of sending me a high-resolution image that I can use.

I am grateful to all my teachers at the Film Studies Department of Jadavpur University and my thesis supervisor Professor Sanjoy Mukhopadhyay for helping me out with books and ideas during my research days.

Maa and Baba for just being there for me.

Soumya, Smriti, and Tista for their constant encouragement. Arinjoy for being so funny.

And Debabrata, my devil's advocate, and my copy editor, who made me fall in love with films back in 2006.

Introduction

"Live Forever by Dying Today": Taxidermy, Corporeal Gothic, and Alfred Hitchcock's *Psycho*

An agent for the Liquor Control Department, Johnson, takes shelter in the bizarre Cuckoo Bird Inn where he must protect himself from its owner, Mrs. Pratt, and her demented caretaker and taxidermist, Harold, or else he will end up being a stuffed specimen himself in Bert Williams' 1965 film, *The Nest of the Cuckoo Birds*.

In Jose Larraz's exploitation film *Deviation* (1971), a taxidermist (with a special interest in tattooed skin) and his sister keep a house of drugs and orgies where there is rampant use of bodies engaged in violence, murder, and sex.

A physically vulnerable self-deluding taxidermist dreams of a perfect crime in Fabián Bielinsky's *The Aura* (2005).

Snubbed by his father for being a "carcass stuffer," taxidermist Lajoska Balatoni seeks immortality by gradually converting his own live body as a taxidermized specimen by gutting his organs one after another in György Pálfi's flesh fest *Taxidermia* (2006).

Obsessed by the "beauty of decay," serial killer Jack practices human taxidermy to forge "a newly credible human being" labeling his acts of destruction as a new form of creativity in Lars von Trier's *The House That Jack Built* (2018).

Rosie and Miles, two pre-teens, on their way to watch the July 4 fireworks, are attacked by a taxidermist, and parts of the dead specimens scattered in the barn become part of their nightmarish struggle for survival in Austin Rourke's short film *A Strange Calm* (2020).

An obese lonely taxidermist kills and stuffs a waitress, typically slasher-style, to own her forever in Aaron Rowe's short film *Bondo* (2020).

"Live Forever by Dying Today" is an advertisement posted on the Internet by a taxidermist which leads to a bizarre love story between the taxidermist and her future specimen who craves immortal youth by agreeing to die now and live forever in Theo Rhys' *Stuffed* (2021). She consoles herself by singing, "Don't forget he's just flesh and leather, a dream I want to fill."

Evil, self-delusive, and usually the villain of the piece, taxidermists are bad news in films. They are usually associated with unhealthy obsessions. They are artists trapped in their fantasies, seeking permanence in objects perishable. Gutting a body, preserving its skin, and rearranging it to make a replica of its previous live form are to many an eerie art. This leads to the convenient association between taxidermists and grotesqueness. Alfred Hitchcock (1899–1980) is perhaps the first filmmaker in mainstream narrative cinema who exploits this connect in *Psycho* (1960). Post-*Psycho*, we find a steady flow of films that draw a straight line between taxidermy and grotesqueness. The films in trying to demonize taxidermists, however, bring forth a unique aspect of such practitioners—no other artist (apart from an embalmer) has such an intimate knowledge of the visceral vulnerability of her raw material. Hence, it is tempting to employ taxidermy and taxidermists as common tropes in Body Horrors. Alfred Hitchcock's *Psycho* does just that.

Psycho starts with the story of a first-time-thief and real estate secretary, Marion Crane (Janet Leigh), who steals 40,000 dollars from her employer's client, runs away from Phoenix to meet her partner at Fairvale, stops at a roadside motel and gets murdered by its owner, a psychotic killer, Norman Bates (Anthony Perkins), who has also killed and taxidermized his mother. Critics dismissed the plot as trivial; Paramount was skeptical about the project, and the prevalent Hays Code did not approve of the nudity and scatological content of the film. Hitchcock, nevertheless, took the plunge. He produced the film with Paramount having a meager share. The film was made on a shoestring budget with only Bernard Hermann (music director) and Saul Bass (title designer) as expensive recruits. It was shot in black and white with his television crew and the entire shooting was completed in forty-two days.

The film proved to be a huge commercial success as it grossed about fifteen million dollars. Hitchcock became one of the most powerful and successful filmmakers in Hollywood, and *Psycho* presaged a new genre in Hollywood—the slashers. The film became a cult creation with its infamous shower scene replicated (directly or obliquely) several times by other filmmakers.[1] The slashing (of Marion Crane) is something that Hollywood had not witnessed before. It was sudden, it was brutal, and it was audacious as Hitchcock had killed off his leading lady with more than half of the film's screen time remaining. These bold steps of Hitchcock perhaps shifted our attention away from another significant character of the film—Norma Bates,[2] the mother of Norman Bates. Norma is a taxidermized corpse killed and preserved by her son who suffers from an overidentification with his mother so much so that he kills attractive young women in her name.

Hitchcock's *Psycho* is based on Robert Bloch's 1959 horror fiction of the same name, which in turn was inspired by the actual findings in the obscure house of a man named Ed Gein in Wisconsin. The story (or the actual event) runs thus: after the mysterious disappearance of a local woman, investigators search the house of Ed Gein and discover

> [a] human skin purse and bracelets ... A tom-tom rigged from a quart can with skin stretched across the top and bottom ... The eviscerated skins of four women's faces, rouged, made-up, and thumbtacked to the wall at eye level ... A rolled-up pair of leggings and skin "vest," including the mammaries, severed from another unfortunate.
> (*The Making of Psycho*, Rebello 1990, 3)

Out of these raw materials Hitchcock fleshes out his most prominently corporeal Gothic film.

---

[1] Brian De Palma's *Dressed to Kill* (1980) and *Blow Out* (1981), John De Bello's parody *Killer Tomatoes Strike Back* (1991), and Gus Van Sant's shot-by-shot remake titled *Psycho* (1998) are a few instances.
[2] Going against popular practice I deliberately choose to write "Norma Bates" instead of "Mrs. Bates" because in the climax of the film Norman, about to attack Lila, enters shrieking "I am Norma!!!" (Joseph Stefano's script 1959). This screaming of her name, the final assertion of her identity, ironically through her son, gets drowned by Bernard Hermann's screeching chords and Lila's scream.

An overview of canonical criticisms and theories on Alfred Hitchcock shows a trend of theoretical oversight (or, at least, understatement) of the elements of corporeality in his films. Hitchcock's films have largely been viewed through the historicist, feminist psychoanalytic, and Marxist lens. To the French cinephiles of the 1960s and 1970s, Hitchcock was a profound modernist thinker and a great manipulator of form.[3] While Claude Chabrol and Eric Rohmer see him as a philosopher of the "Kantian mode," Jean Douchet argues that it is the "intellectual world" of the "Hitchcockian oeuvre" that enables his viewers to transcend the baser aspects of the body. While recognizing the importance of terror in Hitchcock films, Douchet however argues that terror is "not the ultimate goal pursued by Hitchcock." He assigns a "mission" to Hitchcock's "suspense": "And this mission is cathartic. The spectator has to 'undo his repressions' in a psychoanalytical sense, confess himself on a logical plane, purify himself on a spiritual level" ("Hitch and His Public" 2009, 17). Speaking of *Rear Window*, Douchet labels feelings of desire and fear that are aroused by Hitchcock as "low" and "vile": "Hitchcock first excites vile and low feelings in his public" that can only be transcended later with the aid of the intellectual world, "devoid of any passion, detached from subjectivity, freed of all unhealthy curiosity" (2009, 22). William Rothman in *The Murderous Gaze* (1982) approaches Hitchcock films primarily from the perspective of authorship. In his recent work *Must We Kill the Thing We Love?* (2014), he attempts to unearth the moral dimensions in Hitchcock thrillers by aligning them with classical Hollywood "comedies of remarriage." He reads Hitchcock's films through the prism of "Emersonian perfectionism."[4]

The role of visual experience, and its complex relationship with the self, constitutes a major body of feminist reading of Hitchcock's films. In trying to show the mainstream narrative films' reduction of women into passive objects of male voyeurism, Laura Mulvey's *Visual Pleasure and Narrative Cinema* (1975) speaks of the centrality of vision in cinematic experience by analyzing

---

[3] According to Rohmer and Chabrol, "Hitchcock is one of the greatest inventors of form in the entire history of cinema ... an entire moral universe has been elaborated on the basis of this form and by its very rigour. In Hitchcock's work form does not embellish content, it creates it" (Quoted by Haeffner 2005, 45).

[4] Rothman explains that for Emerson "thinking has a moral dimension." He states: "The thought that we must walk in the direction of the unattained but attainable self, that this is the path toward freedom, is the heart and soul of Emersonian perfectionism" (5).

films like *Rear Window* (1954), *Vertigo* (1958), and *Marnie* (1964). Mulvey looks at the films as a choreography of looks based on the active male/passive female binary. She takes Freud's ideas of scopophilia to explain how gendered Hitchcock's films are. The female body, according to Mulvey, is projected as an object of male desire, and women as well are forced into compulsory male spectatorship. Mulvey's idea of gaze, based on Freud, focuses on the gaze of the subject (male spectator), while Zizek in "In My Bold Gaze My Ruin Is Writ Large" (1992) looks at Hitchcock's films through Lacanian psychoanalysis (the gaze of the Other). William Rothman, on the other hand, speaks of the gaze of the camera in *The Murderous Gaze* (1982). Hitchcock's films, in these insightful pivotal studies, are critiqued by how the camera looks at the characters, how the characters look at each other, and how we are asked to look at them. If we shift our focus from these cognitive considerations of Hitchcock's films to a more corporeal deliberation, we find Paul Elliott's seminal work *Hitchcock and the Cinema of Sensations* (2011), where he applies an alternative form of film-reading based on the theory of embodied spectatorship. Elliott contributes significantly to Hitchcock studies by exploring how his films appeal to our sensory organs. Applying the theory of "postmodern scopic regime,"[5] he reads scenes from Hitchcock films to show how our embodied (or sensory) experiencing of a film plays a crucial role in understanding a film. Elliott's work, therefore, foregrounds the corporeality of people, both on-screen and off-screen, as a significant concern of a Hitchcock film.

Psycho and Corporeal Gothic

The corporeal Gothic and Hitchcock's films are as much concerned with the uncanny preservation of life and the body as with the death or destruction of the human being and the human body. *Psycho* is one of the few Hitchcock films

---

[5] The term "scopic regime" is used in opposition to the idea that vision is universal. Sight and the ways of seeing are culturally constructed. Postmodern scopic regime disagrees with an ocularcentric reading of films and argues that sight is a synesthetic experience and cannot be dissociated from the other perceptual processes of the body. Sight is merely one among many perceptual routes, each of which contributes significantly in enriching our understanding of ourselves and experiencing the world around us. Elliott does not use the term "postmodern" in a strictly temporal sense. The term "postmodern" is used to depict a shift from modernist ideas of the "grand narrative of vision and the autonomy of the senses" (Loc 902).

that deal with Gothic corporeality. The dark and stormy night, the demented old lady, a psychotic killer, the abundance of secrets, and a menacing setting have usually been discussed while speaking of the grim atmosphere of *Psycho*. Stephen Rebello, for instance, concentrates on "such creaky elements as the rattletrap Old Dark House, the stormy night, and the crackpot madwoman locked in the dank basement" (1990, 12); Patrick McGilligan speaks of "a phantasmagoria with a scary mansion, stairwell, and dark basement; it was a Peeping Tom and a screaming Jane; it was the world's worst bathroom nightmare, mingling nudity and blood" (2003, 579). The preserved corpses, however, do not find a place in such an enumeration of Gothic features. The contribution that the present volume attempts to make to an already existing rich field of Hitchcock scholarship is a taxidermy-centered re-reading of the films of Alfred Hitchcock and to understand the place of *Psycho* (where taxidermy forms a major motif) in the cinematic continuum of horror films.

The Gothic connotations of taxidermy have been effectively employed by Hitchcock in *Psycho* at a time when both taxidermy and horror films were at their lowest ebb in popular culture. *Psycho* plays the crucial role of reviving Body Horrors in the form of later-day slasher films of the late 1960s and 1970s. Significantly, the late 1960s and 1970s were also times when taxidermy received a new lease of life. It gradually became a popular art form and remains so to date. The present volume places Hitchcock at the crux of a major shift in the filming of female bodies in horror films. It attempts to give feminist reading a new tool to explore the art of reconstruction of an ephemeral body in Hitchcock's films: taxidermy—real and metaphoric. One of the chief analytical tools of this book is the situating of *Psycho* and other post-1950 Hitchcock films, after a detailed historical analysis of taxidermy (with special emphasis on Victorian taxidermy), within the discourse of that art. Applying feminist reading to the art of destruction and reconstruction of a transient body, the book explores the crucial role of taxidermy in Hitchcock's *Psycho* and its metaphoric presence in some of his other darker creations.

The threat of a body spiraling out of control, the urge to tame, contain, and re-fashion it, and finally to preserve that tamed, contained, re-fashioned re-creation for as long as possible are the three major concerns that form the common grounds of corporeality as they feature in Body Horrors, and in the films of Alfred Hitchcock. Longing, destruction, and preservation with their attendant preoccupation with the past, the dead, and the fleeting are the stimuli that inform creators of such texts (both in literature and in films). Taxidermy is used by Hitchcock in *Psycho* in ways that bring forth such nuances that we usually associate with this art of corporeal preservation.

Psycho and Taxidermy

Taxidermy, derived from the Greek words "*taxis*" and "*derma*," literally means "arrangement of the skin." The art of arranging and/or rearranging the skin of a dead animal over a manikin to re-create a body as an exhibit or a trophy or perhaps a site of memory, longing, and nostalgia is how one can define taxidermy. Melissa Milgrom in *Still Life: Adventures in Taxidermy* (2010) focuses on the ambivalent reactions that the recreated corpses evoke in us. Rachel Poliquin in *The Breathless Zoo* (2012) speaks of the emotions of longing and mourning that accompany these specimens frozen in time. Donna Haraway in *Primate Visions* (1989) speaks of the power relations at work in the entire enterprise of acquiring exotic specimens from distant lands and hailing them as a colonist's trophy. Michelle Henning in *Anthropomorphic Taxidermy and the Death of Nature* (2007) and Conor Creaney in *Paralytic Animation* (2010) speak of Victorian anthropomorphic taxidermy that sheds light on the nineteenth-century understanding of human and nonhuman bodies and their often-complex relationship.

The more recent works of Gregory and Purdy ("Present Signs, Dead Things," 2015), and Racheal Harris (*Skin, Meaning and Symbolism in Pet Memorials*, 2019) speak of ethical taxidermy that focuses more on the aspects of love, loss, and admiration as motivations behind such conservations. While Gregory and Purdy concentrate on works of contemporary taxidermists like Polly Morgan and Emily Mayer, Harris looks at the art of inking and the art of taxidermy as intimately associated with touch experience. Such wide-ranging scholarly works show the myriad implications inherent in the entire process of preservation. Contemporary taxidermy, unlike Victorian taxidermy, does not usually force the corpse of an animal to imitate human actions, nor does it veil the dead body with life-like postures; present taxidermy installations often celebrate the very deadness of the animal. Preservation no longer means the preservation of a semblance of life; rather it is the preservation of the material remains of a body without the forced performance of a mock life.

Within the discourse of animal studies, while Poliquin and Haraway speak of the power relations that invade the practice of taxidermy; Alberti, Gregory, Purdy, Henning, and Harris speak of nostalgia and melancholia that pervade such creations. Reading skin—the basic ingredient of taxidermy—and its numerous subtexts are carried out by all these scholars. It cannot be denied that scholars who write of taxidermized bodies mildly fictionalize bodies that evoke fear, awe, fascination, and love. *Psycho* may be termed a landmark film that contains the major aspects of the art of taxidermy as discussed by these experts—from trophies and exhibits to loss, nostalgia, and longing. Melissa Milgrom begins her book *Still Life* (2010) by quoting Norman Bates, "My hobby is stuffing things—you know, taxidermy." Again, Poliquin mentions the function of taxidermy in *Psycho* as a "queasy sign of psychological decay" (2012, 38). But there is more to the use of taxidermy in *Psycho*. The recreated corpse of Norma Bates and the birds stuffed and mounted in the Bates motel parlor are a filmic re-telling of all that taxidermy stands for—a hollowed-out version of times past that haunt all the major characters of the film—Norman, Marion, Lila (Vera Miles) and Norma Bates.

Norman Bates stuffs birds to "fill" his "empty" time. Art that deals with hollow structures and dead skin that look alive is a perfect art for a man with a hollow life, a life that he seeks to stuff with the skin of his mother, and strives throughout his life to make that skin look alive. Longing and fetishism may be seen as two motivations behind Norman's stuffing of birds and more significantly his preserving of his mother. His longing to see his mother alive is so acute that he becomes his mother at times. *Psycho* is one of the rare instances of taxidermy where the creator empties himself into his creation.

The use of taxidermy in *Psycho* is mentioned by Hitchcock scholars like Stephen Rebello in *Alfred Hitchcock and the Making of Psycho* (1990), Raymond Durgnat in *A Long Hard Look at Psycho* (2002), and Donald Spoto in *The Dark Side of Genius* (1999). Spoto speaks of the significance of avian imagery in *Psycho* and *The Birds* and points out Hitchcock's deliberate replacing of animal stuffing in Robert Bloch's novel *Psycho* (1959) with bird stuffing in the film, bringing forth the significant analogy of birds and women in his films. David Greven, in his queer reading of *Marnie* in *Intimate Violence* (2014), speaks of another significant feature of Hitchcock films that can be obliquely connected to the motif of taxidermy—"life-in-deathness," "the lifeless yet antic merry-go-round horses in *Strangers on a Train*, and the death mother in *Psycho* ... the trope of life-in-deathness, which evinces the influence of Edgar Allan Poe, is no less significant in the later film" (202). The only detailed study of the use of taxidermy in *Psycho* is found in Miran Bozovic's essay "Of 'farther uses of the dead to the living': Hitchcock and Bentham" (2004), where the author attempts to draw a parallel between Norman Bates' practice of taxidermy and Jeremy Bentham's idea of "autoiconization." Bozovic in this chapter looks at the human body and its preservation through the lens of utilitarianism. However, the article concentrates more on Bentham and his views on the auto-icon ("a man who is his own image," Bentham quoted by Bozovic 2004, 248) and how the dead can be of use to the living. *Psycho*, in this chapter, serves as an example of how human taxidermy has been useful for its practitioners. Taxidermy as a highly polysemic art is not the subject of this article. Moreover, one major difference between Bentham's preserved body and that of Norma Bates is that Bentham *willed* his preservation. His body was a gift to the living beings whereas Norma Bates is a victim of her son's perverse urge to preserve her remains. Thus, the crucial element of power relations that form a major strain in taxidermy is not the concern of Bozovic's chapter. How the art of taxidermy impregnates *Psycho* with possibilities of horror does not figure in these works. *Psycho* and its threads of taxidermized bodies with Gothic potentials, therefore, wait to be tied together.

Psycho, Victorian "Abhumans," and "Humanimals"

The nineteenth century, and its "thing" culture, witnessed a surge of anthropomorphic taxidermy where animal corpses were refashioned to imitate human actions and stances. They were made to participate in human narratives of myths and folklore. The dead animals who were re-created in the image of humans by anthropomorphic taxidermists such as Hermann Ploucquet, Walter Potter, and Charles Waterton may be described by the term "humanimals" caught up as they are between animal bodies and human actions. The nature of functions the "humanimals" were made to perform was not, however, the same for all the anthropomorphic taxidermic creations. In the case of Hermann Ploucquet's taxidermy, the overriding feature was that of humor that "stems from an understanding of a rigid hierarchy that the animals are supposedly breaking" ("Paralytic Animations," Creaney 2010, 15). However, "in [Potter's] tableaux the overlaying of human behavior onto animal bodies is no longer primarily 'ludicrous'; rather it asserts a profound similarity between the human and animal worlds … the effect of having individualized, realistic identities" (Creaney 2010, 15).

Significantly, the late nineteenth century also witnessed a proliferation of Gothic literary texts that problematized the human/nonhuman binary. By rummaging through the myriad labyrinths of a highly complex physical constitution of the human subject, the authors of the Gothic texts obliterate the reassuring lines between familiar and unfamiliar, fantasy and nightmare, progression and regression, giving birth to characters like vampires, werewolves, ape-men, and beast-people, perching on the precarious strands of fluid forms. Kelly Hurley in *The Gothic Body: Sexuality, Materialism, and Degeneration at the Fin de Siècle* (1996), discusses the proliferation of "abhumans" that populate the British Gothic narratives at the turn of the century: *The Hunting of the "Soko"* (1881), *The Strange Case of Dr. Jekyll and Mr. Hyde* (1886), *The Weapons of Mystery* (1890), *The Great God Pan* (1894), *The Island of Dr. Moreau* (1896), *Dracula* (1897), *The Beetle* (1897), and so on.

The idea of retracing the stages of evolution is clearly shown in H. G. Wells' *The Island of Dr. Moreau* (1896). The novel is the harrowing tale of Prendick who is rescued at sea and is brought to the dystopic island of Dr. Moreau where through vivisection Dr. Moreau tries to recreate beasts into humans, giving rise to a peculiar breed perched on human/nonhuman liminality. They are tortured and controlled by the forbearing Moreau, until one day his creations revolt against him and kill him. Prendick, already nauseated by such gross attempts of Moreau, manages to escape, and returns to his land, only to be haunted by his nightmarish past, his idea of a clear human/nonhuman divide shattered forever. After witnessing the transformation of animals into humanimals⁶ on the island, Prendick, after his return home, starts noticing animal gestures and poses in humans:

> I could not get away from men; their voices came through windows; locked doors were flimsy safeguards. I would go out into the streets to fight with my delusion, and prowling women would mew after me, furtive craving men glance jealously at me, weary pale workers go coughing by me, with tired eyes and eager paces like wounded deer dripping blood .... Then I would turn aside ... into some library, and there the intent faces over the books seemed but patient creatures waiting for prey. Particularly nauseous were the blank expressionless faces of people in trains and omnibuses; they seemed no more my fellow-creatures than dead bodies would be, so that I did not dare to travel unless I was assured of being alone. And even it seemed that I, too, was not a reasonable creature, but only an animal tormented with some strange disorder in its brain, that sent it to wander alone, like a sheep stricken with the gid.
>
> (2005, 138–9)

The soft and yielding carcasses of the animals in a nineteenth-century anthropomorphic installation, like Dr. Moreau's "samples for vivisection," were used as bodies that were molded to imitate human actions and behaviors. This intermingling of dead/alive, and animal/human bring forth the idea of permeability of the living corporeal form. The irony in both taxidermy and the corporeal Gothic is their desperate attempt to achieve wholeness and stability with raw materials (the skin and the body) that are themselves given to fragmentation and permeability. A taxidermist may be defined as one who searches for permanence in perishable objects. He may be termed as "a speculator in perishables" (a phrase that Hitchcock uses to describe himself in *It's Only a Movie* 2005, 58).

The Victorian age is perhaps the most appropriate time to explore the interstices shared by the art of taxidermy and Gothic texts since it was a time

---

[6] Kelly Hurley borrows the term "abhumans" from Hodgson to describe the human bodies that at the turn of the century destabilized the idea of human normativity (1996, 3). In the present context in which I try to describe the animals that are captured and re-created by Dr. Moreau in the images of humans, the term "humanimal" has been used. The term may also be applied to all those anthropomorphic taxidermy animal forms that are made to imitate humans as they mimic human postures and participate in human narratives.

when Charles Darwin published his *On the Origin of Species* (1859). After this path-breaking work of Darwin and after the publication of T. H. Huxley's *On the Physical Basis of Life* (1869) nonhumans and humans, for the first time in the human psyche, had come to a dangerous proximity. Anthropomorphic taxidermy and Gothic monsters of the late Victorian age are testaments to the anxieties arising out of the emerging discourses on the theories of evolution and devolution. Victorian society is rife with instances of "humanimals" and "abhumans" who constantly interrogate and challenge the idea of a fixed and stable physical form. This amalgamation of opposites, a blend of contradictions, a fading of rigid categories, and the fluidity of anatomy, are explicated a century later in the world of films by Alfred Hitchcock in *Psycho* where the body of Norma Bates and Norman Bates become melting pots of myriad contradictory anatomies.[7]

Fin de Siècle Gothic Literature and Body Horrors of Twentieth-Century Cinema

The publication of Judith Halberstam's *Skin Shows: Gothic Horror and the Technology of Monsters* in 1995 is a significant work that initiates a comparative study between the neo-Gothic late Victorian literature and the Body Horrors of twentieth-century cinema. Halberstam begins her study of skin in Buffalo Bill's basement (Jonathan Demme's *The Silence of the Lambs*, 1991). By studying Buffalo Bill as the archetypal monster (much in the vein of Frankenstein's Creature), she attempts to forge a link between the "monsters" of the present age and "monsters" of late nineteenth-century Gothic fiction. Halberstam speaks of the skin of flayed women that Buffalo dons. A study of this skin, Halberstam argues, defines and redefines the category of "normal"

---

[7] Alfred Hitchcock born in London in 1899 was heavily influenced by the Victorian world and its aesthetics. He was also an avid reader of late Victorian literature. See Paula Marantz Cohen's seminal work *Alfred Hitchcock: The Legacy of Victorianism* (1995). While Cohen speaks of the ideological trends and the Victorian model of the nuclear family in Hitchcock's films and his life, my focus is on the Victorian display culture and its effect on Hitchcock, specifically his use of the art of taxidermy—literal and figurative—in his works.

anatomy. Skin plays a crucial part in culturally constructing the shifting ideas of normativity.

Halberstam's attempt of connecting neo-Gothic tales of the *fin de siècle* with twentieth-century horror films draws our attention to the slashers/exploitation/horror films that were making their presence strongly felt from the late 1960s. This mainstreaming of horror in visual culture brought forth several scholarly works that aimed at elevating horror as a legitimate subject to be brought within serious academic consideration. Horror and its visceral affect, conventionally associated with low culture, had, since the 1990s, been legitimized through the scholarly works of Steven Bruhm, Linda Williams, Philip Brophy, Steven Shaviro, Jack Morgan, Catherine Spooner, Xavier Aldana Reyes, and Marie Mulvey-Roberts to name a few.

Xavier Aldana Reyes in *Body Gothic: Corporeal Transgression in Contemporary Literature and Horror Film* (2014) begins by defining what Body Gothic is: "Body Gothic gives prevalence to texts that have been ignored by critics, often because they have been deemed unintellectual or shlocky, and which expose the prevalence of a grotesquerie and explicitness that I read as part and parcel of the gothic" (Reyes 2014, 2). By exploring key texts in splatterpunk, body horror, the new avant-pulp, the slaughterhouse novel, torture porn, and surgical horror, Reyes analyses the explicit graphic violent side of the Gothic. Reyes reiterates the idea that the Body Gothic "relies on the readers'/viewers' awareness of their bodies, particularly of their vulnerability and shared experience of projected pain through vicarious feelings" (2014, 1–2). Reyes' work is important in the context of cinema spectatorship as it reads the genre of the Body Gothic as one that exploits the body of the viewer/reader as an index of response, as well as a site of reception where the body becomes an active participant in understanding visual and literary texts.

While Xavier Aldana Reyes argues that "[t]he gothic is experienced in the flesh, in its surfaces and crevices, and thus reveals its inherent and universal inscriptibility" (2014, 50), Marie Mulvey-Roberts in *Dangerous Bodies: Historicising the Gothic Corporeal* (2016) speaks of those Gothic inscriptions on the bodies of the monsters, the others on whose flesh are inscribed the histories of religious fanaticism, racism, chauvinism, and anti-Semitism. Mulvey-Roberts states, "[t]he making of the Gothic world, as for any repressive institution or state, depends upon the consensual formation of a monstrous alterity, whether it be vampire, ghost, demonic stigmatic or man-made monster" (2018, 3). Monstrosity or otherness in Mulvey-Roberts' work makes its stark appearance through corporeality. Mulvey-Roberts attempts to unearth the true horrors underlying such fictional narratives of desecration and destruction. She takes Mary Shelley's *Frankenstein* (1818), Horace Walpole's *The Castle of Otranto* (1764), Matthew Lewis's *The Monk* (1796), Bram Stoker's *Dracula* (1897), and F. W. Murnau's film *Nosferatu* (1922) as case studies to show how monastic institutions, slave plantations, operation theatres of the men of medicine, concentration camps, anti-Semitism, and battlefields are the breeding grounds of such monsters. Through her reading of institutional and social oppression, she brings forth the idea that monsters are carefully and meticulously crafted: "[a]s the fleshed-out ghost of history" (2018, 4).

Fred Botting in *Limits of Horror: Technology, Bodies, Gothic* (2008) explores, on the other hand, the impact of modern technology and media on present-day Gothic. Monster—that is, the other against whom the self is usually defined, at present has lost its menacing impact as s/he no longer remains a figure of aberration but has been gradually absorbed and assimilated within the mainstream. Society teems with the monstrous so much so that the demarcating lines between the center and the margin have been smudged: "The acceptance of the vampire, the embrace of deformity and surgical alteration, and the understanding of the body as artifice leads to a loss of distinction; as such, the monster is no longer a figure of difference, and thus no longer monstrous" (Botting 2008, 171). Taking a cue from Fred Botting we may add that at a time when the menace of decorporealization in a world of cyber-reality is threatening to eclipse or overwhelm ideas of the body, at a time when monstrosity and deformity are struggling to remain conspicuous, all these critical approaches to the corporeal Gothic have helped in establishing a counter-narrative that situates the body squarely at the center of the genre. The various strands of these critical works have helped shape the arguments of this book and its attempt at situating Hitchcock's *Psycho* squarely within the genre of the corporeal Gothic.

The studies on corporeal Gothic explore several aspects of the body: deformity, liminality, alterity, and grotesqueness. They speak of destruction, desecration, mutilation, fragmentation, dismemberment, and immolation. There remains one more aspect of the corporeal gothic—an attempt at preservation—that still requires some integration with the Body Horror. While the mainstream attempts to preserve its dominant ideologies either by annihilating or taming and assimilating the aberrant bodies, the deviant bodies, on their part, stubbornly adhere to their nonconformity and reject such ideas of accommodation to posit a counter-narrative that celebrates transgression and excess. The body, therefore, becomes a site of struggle, a potent locus, whose destruction/transformation/preservation becomes crucial in a Body Horror.

The bodies that adhere to contemporary social prescriptions and the bodies that do not are locked up in a perpetual battle. This battle is as much a battle of destroying the other as it is a struggle for preserving the self and preventing it from being subsumed in the other. The reconstructed body of a preserved animal becomes a site of forced performativity, a locus in which the former self battles with its present reconstituted one. The recreated trophies or specimens resonate with the memories of their previous anatomies. This material specter of the past problematizes any superficial reading of the art of taxidermy. The constant war between the form and content of a taxidermized creation engenders endless interpretations that make these objects richer and more ambiguous than the detractors of the art would usually acknowledge.

Fashioning Chapters

In keeping with the subject of this volume, the contents include "bits" and "pieces" and even "chunks" from my previously published articles. In taxidermist's taxonomy, some parts of this book are a "Re-Creation," an "assemblage." Sections of my chapter, "Did he smile his work to see?"— Gothicism, Alfred Hitchcock's *Psycho* and the art of taxidermy" (Mondal 2017), have been used in several parts of the book, especially in Chapters 2 and 4. While "Dead but not Gone: Female body, surveillance and serial-killing in Alfred Hitchcock's *Frenzy*" (Mondal 2019a) forms the basis of my gendered reading of *Frenzy* as a police procedural in Chapter 4, parts of my analysis of *The Skin I Live In* as a surgical horror has been taken from my article "Destruction, Reconstruction and Resistance: The Skin and the Protean Body in Pedro Almodóvar's Body Horror *The Skin I Live In*" (Mondal 2021) in the last chapter.

With Hitchcock's *Psycho* and the art of taxidermy as common threads, the book traces the journey of "remade" skin from the nineteenth century to the twenty-first century, from skin as a vulnerable canvas to be destroyed, reforged, and owned to skin with potentials of resistance and rebellion. While Chapters 1, 2, and 4 have *Psycho* as their main text of concern, the third one concentrates on Hitchcock's other post-1950s grim creations—*Vertigo*, *The Birds*, and *Marnie*. The fourth chapter takes the exhibitionistic violence of *Frenzy* as a point of entry and travels forward to the fifth (and final) chapter that speaks of the almost hackneyed collective cruelty of male monsters in Body Horrors like *The Silence of the Lambs*, *Perfume*, and *The Skin I Live In*. The book traces the "handling" of the female bodies from being taxidermied specimens to installations, from victims of outright slashing to objects of crime fiction and surgical horrors, and ends with the possibility of a body that retaliates.

Taxidermy and its myriad connotations inform all the chapters. Thematically, the first two chapters focus on Victorian "thing culture"[8] and how the taxidermized body of Norma Bates, the art practiced by Norman Bates, and the insularity of the Bates house may be accommodated within Victorian aesthetics. Chapter 1 speaks of the most memorable preserved "specimens" in the history of films—Norma Bates, an exhibit who inspires awe and fear. Chapter 2 concerns itself with spaces of such recreated conservation where the Bates world becomes at once a studio, a workshop, a diorama, and an arrested idyllic museum of Norman Bates where nostalgia and longing reside. Hermann Ploucquet, Walter Potter, and Charles Waterton play significant roles as their creations, their museums, and their curiosity cabinets are used to read the Bates World as a meeting ground of the human and the nonhuman.

---

[8] The Victorian population's penchant for procuring and preserving objects may be termed as Victorian "thing culture." A study of Victorian "thing culture" reads the relationship between subject and object outside the context of a capitalist market system. It applies cultural materialist and new historicist methods to the "things" that feature in Victorian literature, art, and culture. See Asa Brigg's *Victorian Things* (1988).

Chapter 3 speaks of all the insecure men in a Hitchcock oeuvre including himself. *Vertigo*, *The Birds*, and *Marnie* are this chapter's primary texts where men attempt to manufacture "beautiful" "docile" bodies and engage in a futile struggle to eternize the memory of that imagined beauty in a crafted body. Taking a cue from Haraway and Poliquin, the effusion of bird imagery in *Psycho* and *The Birds*, and animal imagery in *Marnie*, the women are shown as exhibits and trophies to be possessed or preyed upon.

Chapter 4 shifts its focus from the films to the filmmaker. This penultimate chapter analyzes *Psycho* as a seminal moment in Hitchcock's oeuvre when his dark humor spirals out of Hollywood's polished control and seeps into the late 1960s and 1970s slasher films that draw their sustenance from unadulterated morbidity. The shower scene and the post-murder set of *Psycho* are read here as sites that evoke uneasiness and, perhaps, shame. Hitchcock is shown as an important figure who unabashedly brings about the filming of gore and female skin that is grabbed with eagerness by the filmmakers of the late 1960s and 1970s flooding the next few years with Body Horrors and exploitation films. Hitchcock's ill-famed shower scene, therefore, places *Psycho* in a tricky relationship with the genre of slashers. The chapter concludes with Hitchcock's *Frenzy*, his penultimate work that can easily be allied to the controversial genre of the slasher. Unlike *Psycho* where violence is staged in the minds of the viewers and cruelty is tempered with a blend of irony and pathos, Hitchcock's *Frenzy* is an all-out lashing, under the garb of a police procedural, at female anatomies as the filmmaker gradually distances himself from the screwball comedies, the spy thrillers and the plights of a wronged man. He moves away from light-hearted banter to a realm of calculated cruelty where the humor does nothing to salvage the morbid grim world he speaks of.

Chapter 5 dwells on the most widely accepted feature associated with the supposedly "kitschy" art of taxidermy—violence. It attempts to delineate a trajectory of Body Horror and locate *Psycho's* place in it. From the dystopic world of *Frenzy* of Chapter 4, the last chapter moves to later cult horrors like *The Silence of the Lambs* (1991), *Perfume: The Story of a Murderer* (2006), and *The Skin I Live In* (2011) where grotesque "creators" are enmeshed in a world of repurposed skin and its myriad conundrums. While their "creations," arrested as coveted specimens and trophies, struggle incessantly to chronicle a counter-narrative of female subjectivity.

While tracing the connection between taxidermy and the trajectory of Body Horrors, the book in no way judges the contemporary practice of taxidermy. The book speaks of pre-Victorian and Victorian taxidermy unless specified otherwise. What I intend to offer here is a take on how we may bring out the less-obvious aspects of taxidermy hidden beneath the palpable violence that the art entails in most mainstream films, particularly in Alfred Hitchcock's *Psycho*. I apply Hitchcock's use of taxidermy to later Body Horrors and while doing so, the bodies of both the "taxidermist" and the "taxidermized" become sites of futile love, anger, grief, and search.

And a lack.

1

Speciesism and Sexism: Norma Bates and Her Victorian Predecessors

"As if I could do anything except sit and stare like one of his stuffed birds"—Norma

In *Psycho* (1960), Alfred Hitchcock constructs one of the most menacing serial killers in film history—Norma Bates—an old, sick, frail, also dead, female killer, taxidermized by her son. This preserved woman is a perfect "recipe" for an abject human body—a corpse that by being taxidermized also embodies the "devalued" aspects of the nonhuman. *Psycho* explicates taxidermy as an art that can bring the dead, the nonhuman, and women on the same platform. Taxidermy is about abject bodies, and Hitchcock through his generous littering of abject bodies in *Psycho* weaves the strands of sexism and speciesism together. The chapter takes the connection between Norma Bates, the house where she is preserved, and the nonhuman multispecies worlds of the tableaus and the miniatures in the curiosity museums of renowned Victorian taxidermists, as an entry point to forge a link between Victorian "thing" culture and Alfred Hitchcock's *Psycho*.

Preserved and/or remade bodies and the art of taxidermy were at the height of their popularity in the nineteenth century. The art of draping and darning the skin of a corpse over a structure (that is either stuffed or hollow) to construct or reconstruct an anatomy that serves as a display piece, a trophy, or perhaps a repository of reminiscence, desire, and wistfulness is how one may define taxidermy. Taxidermy which formed a significant part of Victorian popular culture, and that lost its popularity due to shifting perspectives on anthropocentrism and anthropomorphism, almost a century later, becomes a major motif in a hugely successful Hollywood shocker, Alfred Hitchcock's *Psycho* in 1960.

In the present chapter, Walter Potter's (1835–1918) anthropomorphic installations "The Kittens' Wedding" (1890) and "The Death and Burial of Cock Robin" (1861), and Charles Waterton's (1782–1865) the "Nondescript" (1824)—the three infamous and popular exhibits of nineteenth-century England—are juxtaposed with a twentieth-century weird world peopled by a preserved mother, stuffed birds, an obsessed son, and a looming Victorian mansion. While "The Kittens' Wedding" hails the popular figure of a feline Victorian bride right at the center of its tableau, "The Death and Burial of Cock Robin" brings forth an uncanny tale of death and mourning. Yet again, the "Nondescript" is a grotesque hybrid specimen in tune with the "abhumans" of Gothic literature. These three installations highlight three significant aspects of the Bates world—a taxidermized woman, bereavement, and metamorphic bodies.

Potter's preservation and his careful choreography of birds, kittens, rats, squirrels, and rabbits bring forth the hybrid subjectivities of those mock-alive bodies participating in human narratives. On the one hand, these dead creatures, sitting at a tea table, attending a class, playing cards, or solemnizing a wedding, problematize the anthropocentric complacency that takes the hierarchical division between humans and nonhumans for granted. On the other hand, Waterton's hybrid bodies are quite literally and anatomically liminal ones standing on the threshold of human and not-human as his created creatures (mostly ape-men) are a medley of different quadrupeds assembled to create grotesque specimens one can laugh at. Although such instrumentalized use of nonhuman primates is primarily to satisfy institutional and political resentments on the part of the maker, these hybrid specimens narrate a tale of their own. They open up disconcerting possibilities of a redefinition of self/other relationships that transcend the limiting borders of speciesism. These taxidermized creatures and their resting places that encapsulate within them the binaries of life and death, stillness and movement, tableau and narrative, human and nonhuman, find a complex and grim on-screen representation in the next century in Alfred Hitchcock's weird world of a deranged son, a dead mother, and their dilapidated mansion. The world of *Psycho* by making a taxidermized body the main protagonist of the film and by equating the stuffed birds of the motel wall with the patched-up hollow carcass of a wronged woman interrogates anthropocentric practices. The film forces us to recognize, ironically through preserved cadavers, live human (especially female), and nonhuman bodies as subjective agents. Moreover, this alternative world of the dead, of the nonhuman, of the mad and the aberrant woman critiques, and even at times mocks human-centric geographies, forcing us to think of the alternative possibility of more inclusive biocentric ones that feminist thinkers have long been advocating for.

Stuffed Birds and a Preserved Mother

The connect between speciesism and sexism has emerged as a subject of serious interdisciplinary field of inquiry since the Animal Liberation Movement of the 1970s as evident in the works of Peter Singer (*Animal Liberation*, 1975), Donna Haraway (*Primate Visions*, 1989), Cary Wolfe (*Animal Rites*, 2003), and David Herman (*Narratology beyond the Human*, 2018) to name a few. Singer supports the idea that the ones who are fighting for the rights of Blacks and women should champion the cause of animal liberation as well. Speciesism should be weeded out on the basic principle of equality that should not be applied only to humans. This is an early attempt at bringing racism, sexism, and speciesism together through the leitmotifs of pain and suffering common to all. In "The Politics of Being Female: Primatology Is a Genre of Feminist Theory" (1989), Haraway attempts to forge a coalition between feminism and primatology based on the premise that women and nonhuman primates act as rich sites of remade bodies, or, in Haraway's words "managed" bodies (289). Again, Carol J. Adams in *Neither Man nor Beast: Feminism and the Defense of Animals* (1994) observes that female humans and animals of all sexes constitute subordinate Others to an idealized version of Man in "a Western philosophic tradition that posits women as closer to animals" (11). Later, many scholars of animal studies have drawn our attention from a human-centric to a more biocentric reading of literary and film texts.

Psycho as a text that directly relates speciesism and sexism (stuffed birds and a taxidermized woman) through the practice of corporeal preservation is yet to be discussed. Despite several works that study both literary texts and films through the lens of animal studies, *Psycho* does not figure as part of those discussions. Norma Bates is a figure who combines in her the aberrant Victorian woman confined at the margins of a text or the margins of a house and the asphyxiated nonhuman dead specimens in the curiosity shops and museums. By being a cruel mother, a frail, disheveled woman, she resembles the Miss Havishams, the Miss Sparsits, and the Bertha Masons of the previous century. By being a preserved corpse, she reminds us of all the dead taxidermized figures who formed a part of Victorian drawing room aesthetics. Norma Bates' corpse is a meeting ground of aberrant female human bodies and compliant dead animal bodies. She performs the significant function of highlighting the patriarchal project of accommodating and assimilating women within the class of nonhumans. Norman's treatment of Norma Bates' and Marion's body suggests that the stuffed nonhumans of the motel walls and the luckless women who enter the Bates world are companion species. Both feminism and animal studies scholars may find in Norma Bates a marginalized body that is both dead and alive, young and old, passive and active, human and nonhuman—a corpse preserved in accordance to the masculinist ideals of a son who stuffs "only birds," as he thinks, "only birds look well stuffed because ... they're kind of passive, to begin with" (Norman Bates in *Psycho*).

Psycho's dead Norma Bates who appears to be alive, who appears to be mean, and who appears to be livid, brings to mind one of the most intriguing literary characters of the previous century—Miss Havisham of Charles Dickens' *Great Expectations* (1861): "Now, waxwork and skeleton seemed to have dark eyes that moved and looked at me" (Dickens 2002, 57). This is how Pip describes Miss Havisham. Miss Havisham remains confined in a room where time stands still. Her mansion has not seen the rays of sunlight for decades. It is a place where the past has been mummified, a place where all the clocks have been stopped, a place where the wedding gown of a bride has turned into a shroud of a withered body, a place where the joy of white has given way to the pallor of yellow, a place where spiders and rats run riot over a wedding cake covered with cobwebs. Ninety years later, this forlorn mansion of Miss

Havisham finds its perfect parallel in the menacing tower of a house where Norma Bates and her son reside. Norma Bates' shadow by the window and her silhouette seen through the shower curtain give the viewers a vague glimpse of a woman who physically resembles the old, withered, broken-hearted, bitter Miss Havisham of the previous century. Even after the discovery that Norma Bates is not a live body, but a taxidermized recreation, the similarity persists as Dickens' Miss Havisham in *Great Expectations* is a live body described cadaverously:

> all the things about her had become transfixed ... Her chest had dropped, so that she stooped; and her voice had dropped, so that she spoke low, and with a dead lull upon her; altogether, she had the appearance of having dropped, body and soul, within and without, under the weight of a crushing blow.
> (Dickens 2002, 60)

Miss Havisham's body is a site where life and death cohabit. When Pip describes Miss Havisham, we are left unsure about whether he is speaking of a living body or a decaying corpse:

> I saw that the bride within the bridal dress had withered like the dress, and like the flowers, and had no brightness left but the brightness of her sunken eyes. I saw that the dress had been put upon the rounded figure of a young woman, and that the figure upon which it now hung loose, had shrunk to skin and bone.
> (Dickens 2002, 56)

Her body is like a moving tomb that carries with it all its disappointments, disillusions, and longings. Her body is a stage that constantly and patiently carries out an act of preserving her bitterness, her coveted vengeance, and her futile anger. The rooms where Miss Havisham voluntarily keeps herself confined are in keeping with the death and decay she carts within.

While Dickens gives us a "live" woman who looks almost dead, Alfred Hitchcock offers us a reverse corporeal narrative—a transition from the dead to the "lifelike" in the figure of Norma Bates. While Miss Havisham is a withered body of a "bride," Norma Bates is a decrepit body of a "mother"—two major Victorian female figures. Norma Bates is discovered by Lila and the viewers in *Psycho* in the basement of the Bates house. The basement is a perfect setting for the discovery of Norma Bates: stark, and bare, with an old rickety bunk, a chair where the body is planted, and some old empty wicker baskets littered around. It is dark, cramped, and neglected and looks like a hole where one dumps one's unwanted secrets. This basement carries memories of all the nineteenth-century basements and attics (the peripheral spaces of an abode) where aberrant bodies were kept in confinement, from Bertha Mason in *Jane Eyre* (1847) to Catherine Earnshaw in *Wuthering Heights* (1847) to the Dracula sisters in *Dracula* (1897). Norma Bates carries hints of all these aberrant bodies. When we discover that the body is a dead preserved one, one among many of Norman Bates' collection, that she is no different from the birds perched on the Bates motel wall, we understand that Hitchcock has let the nonhuman and the multispecies world enter his film in a way he has never done before. Destruction, reconstruction, and preservation that form a common thread binding speciesism and sexism do not remain confined to the world of the living but also spread to the world of the dead.

Feline Victorians—Brides and Mothers

Cadavers, hybrid bodies, and liminal identities that were an obsession for the neo-Gothic texts of late nineteenth-century Victorian literature had an uncanny corporeal counterpart in the taxidermized nonhuman corpses that were a rage in Victorian England. One such installation that has the figure of a feline bride eternally arrested at the moment of her marriage is a material and ironical statement on one of the most fascinating Victorian figures—the figure of a Victorian bride frozen forever on the threshold of becoming a wife. Walter Potter's famous installation of twenty dead kittens at a wedding ceremony, named "The Kittens' Wedding" (1890), which formed a significant part of Potter's museum of curiosity in Bramber (Sussex),[1] can be read as an uncanny meeting point between the archetypal Victorian bride, the dead, and the nonhuman.

---

[1] See Pat Morris and Joanna Ebenstein's *Walter Potter's Curious World of Taxidermy* (2014), Conor Creaney's "Paralytic Animation" (2010) and Michelle Henning's "Anthropomorphic Taxidermy and the Death of Nature" (2007) for a detailed analysis of Potter's "The Kittens' Wedding."

Speciesism and Sexism

Figure 1.1 Walter Potter's "The Kittens' Wedding" (1890). Sourced from Alamy.

"[W]ild animals, like unruly human subordinates, could be threatening," explains Harriet Ritvo in *The Animal Estate* (1987, 25). While speaking of the human-animal interaction in the Victorian world, Ritvo speaks of "Good Creatures," "Bad Creatures," and Wild Creatures. A country cat, one of the most debatable pets in history, has been categorically placed in the "Bad Creatures" section (1987, 21). Ritvo points out that a country cat can be placed on the threshold of being "domestic" and "wild" as, despite staying among humans, it "might not even acknowledge that it had a master" (1987, 22). Cats could effectively be compared to "human subordinates" (women, for instance), who could, according to the Victorian populace, be "threatening." They were aberrant bodies who failed "meeting even the minimal standards of obedience" (1987, 21). They consequently became popular mounts at "barn walls and doors" of the gamekeepers' museums (1987, 22), "It was widely agreed that cats were both deceitful and difficult to train. And as the dog's plastic body symbolized its desire to serve, so the cat's body symbolized its stubborn refusal ... the cat resisted the breeders' attempts to modify its appearance" (Ritvo 1987, 21–2). So, one of the sure and convenient ways to tame them was to tame them dead.

Potter's airless glass case with an asphyxiated specimen of a cat bride becomes symptomatic of all the unconventional Victorian brides who refused to meet "the minimal standards of obedience."

Like Miss Havisham's room or Norma Bates' basement, time stands still in Potter's kittens' world. Miss Havisham's mansion and Norma Bates' house, like the miniature cat world mimicking a human wedding, are places where the past has been mummified. The yellowed wedding gown of a perpetually waiting bride in *Great Expectations* finds an ironic parallel in the careful arrangement of jewels, the veil, the brocaded white dress, and the laces of the feline corpse-bride. Again, being dead and being made to stand on two legs, the kittens are forced to mimic human gestures and compelled to participate in a human narrative all the while bearing the burden of a mock life. A dead body forced to sit at the window, made to talk, and forced to participate in the guilt-ridden world of a deranged son is remarkably akin to the dead kittens, who by being dead, have no capacity to resist.

Potter's "The Kittens' Wedding" is an interesting tableau when discussed through the lens of consent theory. The pre-pubescent body of the kitten-bride is an ironic comment on what marriages based on consent were in Victorian society. The very discourse of consent is based on individuals' agency: their autonomy, their maturity, and an informed decision to agree along with the knowledge that one always has the option to refuse. This entire premise on which the pre-requisites of consent stand is rendered ridiculous when an entire *mise-en-scène* of a nuptial ceremony is "peopled" by juvenile kittens. The bodies of these underdeveloped animals participating in a wedding tableau are an acerbic comment on the entire institution of marriage, where, in nineteenth-century England, the bride at least did not have much scope for consent. Her consent based on little or no information was often fractional or completely absent. Force and violence which "The Kittens' Wedding" clearly stages were common occurrences in the lives of several Victorian brides. On the other hand, Miss Havisham is a live body who is a victim of rejection. So compelling is the power of marriage and so dreadful the option of staying alone, that Miss Havisham chooses to remain a victim all her life. Her internalization of the patriarchal ideology that when a man rejects a woman, she becomes a subject of abjection forever, defines her identity. It is this rejection that feeds her victimhood and she refuses to come out of her self-imposed exile. The violence here is implied. The punishment is not self-inflicted as it appears, but rather a consequence of an age-old social stigma that uses the stick of ridicule to belittle a woman who is "not good enough" to be married off. So, Miss Havisham, despite being the owner of Satis House, and despite being affluent, is as helpless and as frozen in time as the kittens. Just like the young kitten bride in the tableau, the old withered human bride *seems* to be willingly residing in a frozen closet. Both remain confined as "brides" waiting to give their consent to become "wives."

But the dead do not give consent. Unlike the Victorian brides and wives like Miss Havisham, Bertha Mason (*Jane Eyre*), or Laura Glyde (*The Woman in White*) the kittens are not alive. They are four times removed from the possibility of consent. Their pre-pubescent anatomies, their nonhuman identities, their state of being dead, and the fact that a Victorian female did not have much scope of giving consent anyway, take away all possible agencies from their bodies. They epitomize abjection. Killed in a neighboring barn, they are marginalized rejected bodies who have been employed by Potter to draw an audience who have a taste for morbid anatomies re-sculpted into pretty acceptable ones. These bodies are tamed, packaged, and humanized to be "dished" out to Victorian visitors who can get a taste of the exotica as their surroundings become increasingly urban and cut off from nature and animals. It is this re-packaging of a dead body where Norma Bates comes in—another body completely devoid of any prospect of consent as she is tamed and packaged for the gratification of an insane son. The glass-enclosed kittens, frozen at a moment where they perform the rituals of a human wedding standing on two legs, wearing morning suits and cream brocade dresses, are highly complex multi-faceted relics of a Victorian visual culture that bring forth the ironies inherent in the relationship between human and nonhuman bodies and between dead and live bodies. Moreover, the blue-eyed feline dead bride with a cream brocade dress and a flowing white veil, about to give her consent in front of a solemn pastor, becomes a corporeal site where the "corpse-like" *Miss* Havisham meets the "supposedly-alive" *Mrs.* Bates.

Unlike the still bride of Potter, Norma Bates challenges the idea of a static mount. The Bates world showcases two types of taxidermy—the birds mounted on a wall who remain static and silent arrested in a kind of "spatial atemporality" (Creaney 2010, 18) and Norma Bates, who despite being a preserved corpse, moves from one space to the other. The preserved birds and the preserved Mother together offer us the ambivalence of the exhibits of a Victorian curiosity museum. While the stuffed birds in their frozen gestures serve as tableaus, Norma Bates' body relates a narrative. The Potter miniature, again, is both a tableau and a narrative (Susan Stewart 1993). Abiding by spatial borders and devoid of speech, they can still embody the fluidity of a tale. The viewer is given access to the simultaneous experience of the material presence of an exhibit and the ceaseless flow of an age-old narrative despite the glass-enclosed airless world that the kittens inhabit. Potter's kittens straddle a "now" and a "forever." As Jane Desmond in "Displaying Death, Animating Life" (2002) states, they might just be a part of "an implied narrative that includes moments 'before' and 'after' that which we see frozen in front of us"—and the exhibits may be in "typical arrested-motion stances" (160). The bride and groom standing on the threshold of wedlock, forever sealed in a state of deferred conjugality, may be read as an ironic statement on the tedium of a heteronormative monogamous human marriage. The tableau through its fixity comments on the dreariness of life stretched endlessly before them—a life, though surrounded by relatives and friends, may not be quite so different from the lonely existence of Dickens' Miss Havisham.

The kittens' glass world in its exclusivity resembles the Bates House. *Psycho* offers us synchronized and often parallel views of two dwellings—the Bates Motel and the Bates House. The Bates House is apparently a hermetically sealed world that forbids outsiders. On the other hand, the motel by definition is a shelter for outsiders. By positioning the demented Norma Bates on a window frame of the house, Hitchcock presents her as a tableau, securely inhabiting her demarcated space, her own "spatial atemporality." But when she comes out to wreak havoc on a space consigned to outsiders, when we are confronted with the violent, fantasized version of a taxidermized body capable to move and kill, we feel the fluidity of the two apparently contradictory spatial boundaries. The body of Norma Bates initiates a story that demands proper closure. Like Potter's feline wedding populace, Norman's birds are safely trapped in the motel office inhabiting a space allotted to them. They are at the same time conveniently available to satisfy our curiosity and feed our squeamishness. It is Norma Bates' supposed capability of disregarding spatial boundaries, her ability to move freely from the house to the motel, that provides us with the necessary exposition leading to a scary conclusion. In Potter's work, the dead are a part of the cultural other, belonging to a lower order, who can conveniently be framed in an ageless miniature form. However, the transcendent uncontaminable form that Potter tries to capture in his kittens is problematized by Hitchcock where Norma Bates does not remain frozen in time. She is a taxidermized body that apparently can move, speak, and actively disturb the onscreen characters and the viewers. She disrupts our complacent affective consumption by refusing to remain framed by the window. Thus, the "mother" does what the "bride" could not.

Macabre Mourning—*Psycho* and "The Death and Burial of Cock Robin"

The act of burying and disinterring the dead is a significant motif of *Psycho*. The body of a young woman is stabbed, buried in a swamp, and disinterred at the end. The body of a dead Mother is unearthed by her son. *Psycho* is not only a film about killing. It is also a film about macabre mourning where the dignity of a dead body is unashamedly flouted. *Psycho*, surfeited with bird images, can be connected to one extremely popular Victorian bird installation of Walter Potter—"The Death and Burial of Cock Robin"—a tableau composed of birds in a grim death service.

This installation made of ninety-eight bird specimens took Potter seven years to complete. Based on the famous nursery rhyme, *The Death of Cock Robin*, the installation was ready to be exhibited in 1861. The rhyme of an anonymous author, with a fair share of macabre detail, goes thus:

> Who killed Cock Robin? I, said the Sparrow with my bow and arrow. I killed Cock Robin. Who saw him die? I, said the Fly, with my little eye, I saw him die. Who caught his blood? I said the fish with my little dish, I caught his blood. Who'll make the shroud? I, said the Beetle, with my thread and needle, I'll make the shroud. Who'll dig his grave? I, said the Owl, with my

pick and shovel, I'll dig his grave. Who'll be the parson? I, said the Rook, with my little book, I'll be the parson. Who'll be the clerk? I, said the Lark if it's not in the dark, I'll be the clerk. Who'll carry the link? I, said the Linnet, I'll fetch in a minute, I'll carry the link. Who'll be chief mourner? I, said the Dove, I mourn for my love, I'll be chief mourner. Who'll carry the coffin? I, said the Kite, if it's not through the night, I'll carry the coffin. Who'll bear the pall? We, said the Wren, both the cock and the hen, We'll bear the pall. Who'll sing the psalm? I, said the Thrush, as she sat on a bush, I'll sing the psalm. Who'll toll the bell? I said the bull, because I can pull, I'll toll the bell. All the birds of the air fell a-sighing and a-sobbing when they heard the bell toll for poor Cock Robin.

Birds and birdsongs, beautiful and harmless as they are, when placed within a violent context, have an eerie potential to augment the violence. This uncanny connection is frequent in Hitchcock films. Hitchcock's *Sabotage* (1936), in fact, has an animated on-screen rendition of the Cock Robin song.

In *Sabotage* birdsongs and spectacles of violence are placed together on several occasions. The film centers around a group of terrorists trying to disturb the peace of London through a bomb blast. The main drama of the film is generated by Mr. Verloc (Oscar Homolka), a cinema hall owner, and his attempt at planting a time bomb at Piccadilly Circus Station in London. Being trailed by the Scotland Yard, he sends his wife's young brother, Stevie (Desmond Tester), to do the job for him. Stevie, who does not know that he is carrying a time bomb with him, gets delayed on his way and dies in the blast. The bomb that constitutes the central crisis of the film is termed "a bird" by the bomb maker who is also the owner of a bird shop. We have three close shots of the coded message "don't forget the birds will sing at 1.45" followed by high-angle shots of a clock that gradually moves toward 1.45 as Stevie undertakes his fateful journey. The final close shot of the message is followed by the spectacle of a blast that kills all the people in a London bus including young Stevie. It was 1.45 and the birds had sung.

When news of Stevie's death arrives, his sister (Sylvia Sidney) who is also Verloc's wife, after discovering her husband's role in the blast, in a state of shock, enters the cinema hall of her husband and watches an animation of "The Death of Cock Robin" being played on screen. The camera focuses on the screen when Cock Robin sings a high-pitched song as the sparrow pierces him with an arrow—an act of random violence coupled with the laughter of the audience that drowns Cock Robin's dying strains. The camera cuts to a close shot of Mrs. Verloc as she is reminded of her brother's meaningless death. She goes back to her husband to serve dinner, and, after a brief hesitation, stabs him as the canary birds of her room start singing. Hitchcock has an uncanny capacity to make scary incidents scarier by adding an element of melancholic beauty to them. The songs of the birds add to the arbitrariness and sadness of the destruction that we witness in *Sabotage* reminding us of Potter's Cock Robin cabinet.

According to the Oxford Dictionary of Nursery Rhymes, the song on the preparation of Cock Robin's burial can be traced back to *Tommy Thumb's Pretty Song Book* (1744). While it was the self-imposed task of the good-hearted Robin to ensure a proper burial for the dead, Potter by arresting the moment of Robin's burial by the other birds in the tableau makes sure that Robin never receives his burial. Ironically, none of the birds participating in the process of the burial receive a proper entombment. The preserved dead birds rather serve as exhibits, as trophies to be displayed.

Potter creates ninety-seven grieving birds about to give Robin a dignified burial Robin deserves. Potter even makes the birds shed tears made of glass beads to amplify their loss. Despite such expressive forms of human grief, Potter's birds in this tableau are anthropomorphic. Unlike "The Kittens' Wedding" where the kittens are made to stand on two legs and made to pretend as humans, here the birds are birds, but they are participating in a ritual prescribed and followed by humans. They are also invested in emotions (the glass-beaded tear drops) that unsettle the viewers. So, they are unmistakably birds who act out the performance of a human burial. Murder, violence, grief, mourning, and a sense of loss, animate an otherwise inanimate tableau. The viewers seem to tumble into a moment where the performers, pierced with grief, are still. This stillness seems to be a temporary stage where the birds pay homage to Cock Robin. The discomfort comes from the fact that this is a never-ending moment of mourning. The stillness is here to stay. They are dead mourners grieving the death of their kin. They are both witnesses of an unexplained murder committed by the sparrow, and testaments of the murders committed by humans. They may even be replicating the actions of a human viewer watching, from outside the glass case, the drama of a morbid death ritual.

Coming to *Psycho*, the body of Norma Bates replicates the cruelty that has been unleashed on her. She is a murdered woman who in turn murders. Such narratives of violence and bereavement carry with them a grim irony—one dead body grieving for itself or for another, and one ravaged body creating another. The birds in the Bates motel office, Norma Bates, and the preserved birds at Cock Robin's funeral are testaments of bullied bodies burdened with the humiliation of a mock life, participating ironically in the drama of their own deaths.

Hitchcock's *Psycho*, like Potter's "The Death and Burial of Cock Robin," offers us a strange narrative of bereavement. Norman Bates, like the mourning birds who have gathered to pay their last respect to the dead Robin, is locked up in his moment of loss, his grief forever deferred. He can never move on, frozen as he is by his own creation. The material presence of Norma Bates renders her absence denied. The entire act of bereavement for the dead one is rendered futile through this creation of a body that by its very presence defeats the purpose of remembrance. The manufacturing of a "docile" body performing and posing in accordance to the whims of its maker, and, in the process, incarcerating the maker in the unpredicted outcome of his craft, is how speciesism and sexism meet in Hitchcock's *Psycho*. And how, ironically, the recreated corpse gets back at its creator.

Hollow Re-creations—Norma Bates and the "Nondescript"

In Hitchcock's *Psycho*, Norma Bates is never played by a "Norma Bates"; she is not even played by Anthony Perkins. Norma Bates in *Psycho*, supposedly projected as Norman while murdering Marion and Arbogast, is an amalgamation of "a variety of doubles, including a female 'Lilliputian'—Her voice is three different people's; one was provided by a man, another by Jeanette Nolan … In her final scene, her voice is a 'collage' of different voices, even within the same sentence" (Durgnat 2002, 14). Thus, Norma Bates is not Norma Bates at all, nor is she, her son. She is constructed through a blend of various bodies and voices; all coming together to create one of the most terrifying serial killers in film history. Norma Bates in *Psycho* is a classic example of what taxidermists term "Re-Creations." Melissa Milgrom in *Still Life: The Adventures of Taxidermy* (2010), while explaining what a "Re-Creation" is, describes a hawk that is not a hawk at all, but a mixture of "turkey, chicken and goose feathers," "[a]ccording to the rule book, Re-Creations are defined as renderings which include no natural parts of the animal portrayed ... For instance, a recreation eagle could be constructed using turkey feathers, or a cow hide could be used to simulate African game" (32–3). Norma Bates is, as a taxidermist would describe, a "Re-Creation," an "assemblage" of the filmmaker.

This process of constructing a character on screen that consists of none of the body parts of the said character reminds us of the methods of an assemblage of another debated taxidermist and conservationist, Charles Waterton, an English Catholic whose Walton Hall was both a museum of curiosities and a haven for birds and animals. Waterton is famous for his odd creations, and one of his most controversial exhibits is the "Nondescript." It is usually believed that in one of his field expeditions in Demerara in 1824, Waterton obtained two howler monkeys. The rear end of one of them was used to create the "Nondescript":

> The Nondescript appears as an odd, roundfaced little man. Waterton accompanied its display with an account of how he had caught this strange creature—which seemed halfway between man and ape—and how he had cut off its head and shoulders and brought it back. In fact, the 'Nondescript' was fashioned out of a monkey's skin—probably the back end of a red howler monkey—and the mouth was probably originally the animal's anus.
> (Henning 2007, 673)

Julia Blackburn in Waterton's biography, *Charles Waterton: 1782–1865: Traveller and Conservationist* (1991), traces Waterton's constant peculiar efforts at confusing and baffling his audience about the truth of the "Nondescript." His accounts, states Blackburn, become increasingly exaggerated and exoticized as he explains the secret of the Creature at its first exhibition in December

Figure 1.2 Charles Waterton's "Nondescript" (1824). Sourced from Alamy.

1824 in Georgetown, in his interview with the local papers, and later in his work, *Wanderings in South America* (1891).[2] Waterton notes with much glee the response of the experts when confronted with this man/ape:

> Some gentlemen of great skill and talent, on inspecting his head, were convinced that the whole series of its features had been changed. Others again have hesitated, and betrayed doubts, not being able to make up their minds whether it can be possible, that the brute features of a monkey can be changed into the noble countenance of a man.
>
> (Waterton quoted by Blackburn 1991, 94)

A discerning audience will finally conclude, a conclusion perhaps hinted subtly by Waterton himself, "that his Nondescript is nothing but a clever fake" (Blackburn 1991, 96). It may just be a "Re-creation" of Waterton, a means to get back at his audience and play with their credulity just as Hitchcock plays with the acute curiosity of an audience eager for a taste of the grotesque and the macabre.

---

[2] See Waterton's *Wanderings in South America* for a detailed description of his adventures in Demerara and his claims of acquiring the "Wild Man" whom he later shapes into the "Nondescript." Available at https://www.gutenberg.org/files/31811/31811-h/31811-h.htm *Wanderings*, released in 2010.

The plot of Hitchcock's film demands two clear on-screen presences of Norma Bates, the murder scene of Milton Arbogast (Martin Balsam) where she stabs him, and when she is carried forcefully by Norman to the basement. While trying to conceal the reality of the mother, and yet not deliberately cheating the audience, Hitchcock resorts to the method of brevity. Hitchcock describes the Arbogast murder scene in the following manner:

> I used a single shot of Arbogast coming up the stairs, and when he got to the top step, I deliberately placed the camera very high for two reasons. The first was so that I could shoot down on top of the mother, because if I'd shown her back, it might have looked as if I was deliberately concealing her face and the audience would have been leery. I used that high angle in order not to give the impression that I was trying to avoid showing her.
> (*Hitchcock/Truffaut* 1984, 273 and 276)

Norman's carrying his mother to the fruit cellar had been executed in the following way:

> I raised the camera when Perkins was going upstairs. He goes into the room and we don't see him, but we hear him say, "Mother, I've got to take you down to the cellar. They're snooping around." And then you see him take her down to the cellar. I didn't want to cut, when he carries her down, to a high shot because the audience would have been suspicious as to why the camera has suddenly jumped away. So I had a hanging camera follow Perkins up the stairs, and when he went into the room I continued going up without a cut. As the camera got up on top of the door, the camera turned and looked back down the stairs again. Meanwhile, I had an argument take place between the son and his mother to distract the audience and take their minds off what the camera was doing. In this way the camera was above Perkins again as he carried his mother down and the public hadn't noticed a thing.
> (*Hitchcock*/Truffaut 1984, 276–7)

Playing with the audience's expectations and keeping them guessing is what the makers of both these "Re-Creations" relish.

When Norma Bates' corpse does appear on screen, we see her as a skeleton covered with skin. Her empty eye sockets and her "lipless grin" show that her eyes and her tongue have been removed. The process is similar to the one followed while taxidermizing a bird (reminding us of Norman's ominous statement, "I only stuff birds"). A dead bird about to be taxidermized is first soaked in borax. The stuffing is made by a mash of wood wool wrapped and fixed, first by thin, and then by thick wires. The body is then dissected, its innards emptied and the legs and wings are then gently pulled off through the skin, leaving the skin and the skull together. This is followed by a flipping of the skin inside out revealing the foramen magnum (an opening at the base of the skull) through which the brain is scooped out followed by the removal of the bird's eyes and tongue. What remains is the skin which is then draped over the structure made of wool wood and stitched up.

However, Norma Bates, beneath her skin and the skeleton seems hollow within. She does not seem to be "stuffed." Her skeleton functions as the form, a manikin, over which her skin is draped and darned.[3] This process somewhat resembles the procedures followed by the eccentric "animal doer," Charles Waterton. While traveling in Guyana, Waterton devised a technique of preservation that was different from that of his contemporary taxidermists. George Harley, a London physician, on his first visit to Walton Hall had called Waterton's specimens as "stuffed," to which Waterton protested, "What do you mean? *Stuffed*, did you say? Allow me to inform you that there are no stuffed animal in this house." He took a preserved polecat and instructed Harley to "[t]ake hold of the head, and hold it firmly." Much to his dismay, Harley recounts: "I did so, when he immediately gave the specimen a sudden jerk and left the head in my hand," Waterton then asked Harley, "Look at the head—what do you see?" "Nothing" was Harley's stunned reply. "Then put your fingers into it, and tell me what you feel," Waterton continues. Harley admits again, "Nothing … No stuffing, no bones, no skull could I either see or feel. It was simply empty. It contained *nothing*" (Blackburn 1991, 176–7). The skin of Waterton's animal about to be preserved was toughened with the aid of chemicals, specially bichloride of mercury, and then molded in a way that ensured an almost genuine and corporeally precise taxidermized exhibit that was otherwise

---

[3] This can only be guessed at after seeing a close shot of Norma Bates in the basement. Neither Norman Bates, nor Hitchcock himself explain the process by which Norma Bates has been preserved. The gaping holes on her face (eye sockets and buccal cavity) help us understand that she is empty within. The skin simply has been patched up and stitched on her skeleton that serves as the basic structure of her preserved body.

hollow inside. Norman Bates' creation of his taxidermized mother seems to be in line with Waterton's method of specimen preservation. Norman Bates departs from Waterton in one significant way. He also preserves the skeleton of his mother over which her skin is pasted. Unlike the birds on Bates' walls, Norma Bates seems hollow within like a Waterton exhibit.

The Monstrous "Abhumans" and Their Makers

Norma Bates has been created as a composite creature on screen by the filmmaker, neither alive nor properly dead, an amalgamation of a medley of bodies and voices. She becomes a peculiarly sinister serial killer, partly because we can, and yet cannot, quite locate or identify her definitely. She arouses in us the same discomfort that we may feel when we encounter a mount like the "Nondescript" who can be identified in parts but whose wholeness somehow eludes us—the mouth is replaced by the anus, the skin is that of an ape, and yet the countenance reminds us of a man. After the publication of Charles Darwin's *On the Origin of Species* (1859) and T. H. Huxley's *On the Physical Basis of Life* (1869) such taxidermy exhibitions of orangutans, chimpanzees, and gorillas mimicking gestures of humans further unsettle viewers, as they bring the fluidity of our species to the fore. The animals become grotesque representations of the human, reminding us of our evolutionary process and the fact that we are not *that* different from them.

The "Nondescript" was also prophetic of the "abhumans"—the human/not-human liminal bodies who crowded the British Gothic narratives at the turn of the century. Kelly Hurley, borrowing the term "abhuman" from Hodgson's *The Night Land* (1912), defines an "abhuman" as a "not quite human subject, characterized by its morphic variability, continually in danger of becoming not-itself, becoming other" (Hurley 1996, 4). The "Nondescript," grotesque in its commingling of the human and the beast, may be seen as a concrete visual representation of Hodgson's abhumans that crowd the *fin de siècle* Gothic narratives. Like the ape-man of R.L. Stevenson's troglodytic Mr. Hyde in *The Strange Case of Dr. Jekyll and Mr. Hyde* (1886), or the blood-sucker of Transylvania in Bram Stoker's *Dracula* (1897), or the beast-humans of

Dr. Moreau's samples of vivisection in H. G. Wells' *The Island of Dr. Moreau* (1896), the "Nondescript" of Waterton is, as Bakhtin puts it in *Rabelais and his World* (1965), "a body in the act of becoming" (1984, 317), a body continually reminding us of our metamorphic malleable corporeality. In *Psycho*, the body of Norman as well as the body of Norma Bates represent the two poles of "becoming"—a constant flux of receding, dying, and being born again—the son emerging out of the mother and the mother grotesquely emerging out of the son, a progression from past to present, and a regression from the present to the past. It is perhaps this reversion from the present to the past that is visually rendered by the last shot of Norman where the living young man dissolves into the old dead Norma. The penultimate dissolve of Hitchcock's camera leaves the narrative in a fluid state, the transformation of one visage to the other is not complete—it captures "the very act of becoming … the eternal, incomplete, unfinished nature of being"; just as Waterton represents his liminal monstrous bodies as "between species: always-already in a state of indifferentiation, or undergoing metamorphoses into a bizarre assortment of human/not—human configurations" that Kelly Hurley speaks of in *The Gothic Body* (Hurley 1996, 10).

Apart from taking a dig at the naïve viewer and the closet taxidermists (Ritvo, *The Platypus and the Mermaid* 1997, 55), the "Nondescript" is also an acerbic attack on the dominant ideology of the time. Being a devout Catholic at a time of Protestant rule, the only way that Waterton could lash out at the mainstream was through the projection of a grotesque abhuman. Waterton voices his resentment against the Protestants and also against contemporary government policies through the creation of a "Nondescript," a "Martin Luther" (a gorilla with donkey's ears), and a "John Bull" (a porcupine in a tortoiseshell with a human face) that epitomize dissidence, that upset our understanding of the world and that wrench our complacency away from us. Physical grotesqueness and the creation of monsters are synonymous with intense aberration from mainstream ideology. As a Catholic, Waterton constantly resisted Protestant ideologies; and as a conservationist, he was distrustful of the rapid industrialization of his society. He chose to rebel against the contemporary government through the creation of "ludicrous" exhibits like the "Nondescript," "Martin Luther after His Fall," and "John Bull and the

National Debt." Again, as a conservationist, he chose to resist the onslaughts of growing urbanization through the nurturing of Walton Hall where owls, weasels, herons, and hedgehogs found a haven amid a teeming nineteenth-century industrial England. We might take an ironic dig at Waterton being labeled as a thorough "conservationist" since his confessions about his actions of killing howler monkeys and the "Wild Man" in Demerara, can be called anything but "conservation":

> Just as he [the Indian guide] left me I heard a rustling in one of the high tufted trees near me. I instantly took aim with my air-gun, and down dropped the animal, lifeless at my feet. Here for the first time I saw the real wild man of the woods.
>
> I looked at him again and again, and was sorry I had ever gone in quest of him. There was no time to be lost … The animal was too large to carry—so taking out my knife I cut off his head and shoulders, threw them on my back, and set off in the direction the Indian had gone—looking up every now and then in the trees behind me to see if I were not pursued by some of their police; for I strongly suspected I had unfortunately killed a man—nor have I yet made up my mind upon the subject.
>
> (*Wanderings* 1891, n.pg.)

Perhaps killing animals (or perchance a man as Waterton himself doubts) outside England did not count as killing, provided he behaved well with the native ones. It is undeniable that Waterton's field expeditions to South America and other locations in search of exotic creatures were not devoid of violence. The monsters he created were often the products of violence and nonconsensual body modifications.

Marie Mulvey-Roberts in *Dangerous Bodies* (2016) traces the etymology of the word "Monstrosity." She states: "Monstrosity derives in part from the Latin verb 'monstrare' ('to show'). Its spectacular derivation points to how the monstrous functions as a looking-glass, permitting us to see our own inner monster and revealing the extent to which monsters are us" (9). The grotesqueness or monstrosity of the "Nondescript" arises from a conflation of the human and animal, and of life and death. It even comes across through a complete inversion of the hierarchy of anatomy (the anus of the monkey is used as the mouth). The "Nondescript" is a statement on the maker's "conflictual identity" as well (Bann 1994, 156), which is intimately related to his creation of monsters. The grotesque is a part of him, the grotesque is used by Waterton as a weapon to ridicule the mainstream as well as to negotiate his identity as an artist of the "abnormal." Norman's conservation, on the other hand, is thoroughly ghoulish. In his attempt to conserve his childhood and his mother, he reveals his inner monster. His resentment for the outer world, for the "institutions" that might take his mother away, make him cling all the more to his created nightmare, his deadly diorama. While the "Nondescript" is a statement on Waterton's identity as a satirist and a nonconformist, Norman's identity overlays, and, at times, mingles with his Creation's identity. But what brings speciesism and sexism together, what brings the howler monkey and Norma Bates together is not only their liminal anatomies, or their unending mock-lives serving their makers' whims, but the viewers' and the makers' encounter with their worst fears perhaps. The two taxidermized figures make us confront our nastiest nightmares: a beast-man, and a mad mother.

Hitchcock, perhaps unwittingly, makes a rare film way before the Animal Liberation Movement of the 1970s, that extends beyond the human body through a human body, to articulate the pain of the nonhuman.

2

Norma's Home and Norman's Diorama: Taxidermy, Longing, and Nostalgia

Psycho and the Synecdochic World of Early Taxidermy

The shores of sixteenth-century Europe witnessed a surge of outlandish creatures brought home from unknown lands. Most of them perished for want of proper preservation and what ultimately reached the continent were broken remnants of exotic nonhuman corpses. Europe was brimming with bits and pieces of such mysterious creatures gleaned from the Americas and brought home by voyagers. Such body parts of unusual animals ultimately rested in the curiosity cabinets of European nature enthusiasts and personal collectors. It was the impoverished state of preservation of such coveted exotic specimens that plagued European collectors all through the sixteenth and the seventeenth centuries. These incomplete pieces of animal anatomy housed in curiosity cabinets seethed with veiled knowledge as out of such small tokens whole new worlds were envisaged. Rather than providing the viewer the complete satiation of knowledge, they lured her further into the labyrinths of the unknown. Such curious specimens became synecdochic representations of a tantalizing world yet to be discovered. They offered the collectors a brief glimpse of a "might-have-been" possession.[1]

Incomplete objects evoke enticing options. They perform as a battle zone highlighting the incongruity between the fantastic tales we associate with them and their place of origin, and the space where they are finally preserved. These

---

[1] The first chapter of *The Breathless Zoo: Taxidermy and the Cultures of Longing* (2012) by Rachel Poliquin provides detailed information about the works of sixteenth- and seventeenth-century European naturalists.

partial tokens placed in living rooms, roadside inns, parlors, and curiosity cabinets alter the spaces that display/house them. They help build a human imaginary that transforms these spaces into repositories of wistfulness or generators of macabre curiosity. The inadequate, half-finished nature of such anatomies, placed amongst everyday household articles, endows an otherwise mundane human construct with numerous possibilities.

Psycho is replete with such incomplete half-glimpsed images of Norma Bates. She is like those broken bits of bizarre creatures brought to the shores of a viewer's imagination, tantalizing and disturbing at the same time. We do not see Norma Bates clearly till the climax in the fruit cellar. We see her silhouette in the shower scene and her shadow on the window frame. Only "bits" of Norma is seen on three occasions in *Psycho* before the climax (the killing of Marion Crane, the stabbing of Milton Arbogast, and Norman's carrying her to the fruit cellar). She is thus never seen clearly, but heard, throughout *Psycho*. Norma Bates, to borrow from Michel Chion, has an "acousmatic presence" (1999, 18).[2]

In the absence of her concrete visual presence, she comes across to us as a voice. But accepting a disembodied voice is difficult for the viewers. We have to create her in our imagination with the help of whichever sensory tool that comes to our aid, just as the sixteenth- and seventeenth-century specimen collectors and nature enthusiasts did. Claws, parts of limbs, tails, and feathers of dead specimens became indexes of whole bodies.

In *Psycho*, Hitchcock does not give us the "whole" of Norma Bates. He provides us with a voice and with a setting where Norma is framed. The setting, that is, the towering house where she resides needs to be ransacked for clues. We enter Norma's room with Lila Crane. It seems we have stepped back into the last century. The four-poster bed, the extravagant dressing table stuffed with satin, an ornamental chiffonier, an elaborate wardrobe, an outsized elliptical full-length pier-glass, satin-covered recamier, and an armchair are where

---

[2] Chion in *The Voice in Cinema* (1999) explains *acousmêtre* as "sound that is heard without its cause or source being seen," an old term revived by Pierre Schaeffer in the 1950s. Chion explicates further, "When the acousmatic presence is a voice, and especially when this voice has not yet been visualized-that is, when we cannot yet connect it to a face-we get a special being, a kind of talking and acting shadow to which we attach the name *acousmêtre*" (19 and 21).

we situate her. We can smell the bygone days in her room. The script reads: "And there is in the room an unmistakably live quality as if even though it is presently unoccupied, it has not been long vacated by some *musty* presence" (Stefano 1959). The whole setting is a reminder of the past century brought forth by the Victorian stuffy decor. Venetian blinds, thick carpet, velvet-covered upholstery, a wide-ranging array of heavy Victorian furnishing, the wardrobe, the crossed bronze hands, the statues, the huge gilded mirrors, and the bed dominating the entire room with Norma's imprint—all create a world where we have traces of her existence but not her actual body. She is there and yet she is not there like parts of early animal tokens that speak of their presence and absence. The "musty presence" that the script speaks of is juxtaposed with creams and cosmetics and perfumes and fresh powders on the dressing table; the dank smell of the traces of a supposedly ill body on the bed is contrasted with the fresh, spotless, well-ironed clothes and shiny polished shoes in the large wardrobe. The space speaks of contrasts, of parts of a lifestyle of a body yet to be discovered. The script reads:

> [Lila] sees the high wardrobe out of the corner of her eyes, goes to it, hesitantly. She opens one door. Fresh, clean, well pressed dresses hang neatly. Lila opens the other door. The sweaters and dresses and robes hang freely, none in moth-proof, storage-type bags. There is even a well-brushed collar of foxes. Along the floor of the wardrobe is a line of clean, polished shoes.
> (Stefano 1959)

Just as the body of Norma is an amalgamation of many opposites, her room is also characterized by similar contrasts; as death co-exists with life in her body, so does the smell of mustiness cohabits with the smell of fresh clothes, toiletries, and new shoes in her room. Reminiscent of the curiosity cabinets and exotica collectors' houses of the sixteenth and seventeenth centuries, in Norma's room two contrasting worlds coexist. Only in this case, the two worlds are separated by time. The audience is invited to create Norma through spatial clues provided by the filmmaker.

In absence of her physical dimension, we take recourse to whatever clues are provided to us by the setting while we try to construct a visual image of her body. We see her thus: she is old; her loose robes, her harsh voice, her disheveled hair, and her sickness, carry with them signs of neglect. The imagined body of Norma "seeps" into us through the "silent registers" of our senses (Marks 2000, 5),[3] as illusory complete bodies may be imagined through a leftover talon or a tail (the rest perhaps being lost at sea). We construct Norma through partially created visual, auditory, and olfactory hints, and the unkempt bed which still carries marks of her corporeal self. The indent made on the bed by Norma's body in her room is a powerful image of the presence of an absence. Presence and absence are locked up in a complex symbiotic relationship in *Psycho* as the clue to the visual presence of the body of Norma points to her actual absence while the absence of the body on the bed apprehends her presence. The indent made on her bed is our first direct interaction with her body without the medium of her victims, Marion and Arbogast, in between. But this body is only a void, an emptiness that Norman fills.

As stated in the previous chapter, Hitchcock plays visual tricks on the audience to hide Norma's appearance. The sound of her voice is another perplexing puzzle that Hitchcock directs at the audience. He almost challenges them to situate that voice in the given temporal and spatial composition. Film sound maintains a consistent balance between volume and distance. It usually has a well-defined source and spatial perspective. We hear Norma's voice three times in the film from varying distances. Though the spatial relations alter in each scene, the gritty, source-less, disembodied quality of the voice remains unchanged. The architecture here does not play any part in molding the voice. When Marion hears Norma's voice for the first time, it seems unreal: a strange echoing voice loud and clear which seems impossible considering the distance between the motel and the house with closed windows and the rain outside.

---

[3] Laura U. Marks in her book on intercultural films, *The Skin of the Film: Intercultural Cinema, Embodiment, and the Senses* (2000) frames an alternative form of film-reading based on the theory of embodied spectatorship. Embodied spectatorship disagrees with an ocular centric reading of films and argues that sight is a synesthetic experience and cannot be dissociated from the other perceptual processes of the body: "I am most interested in meaning that lies outside the means of cinematic signification, namely, visual image and sound, altogether … how film and video represent the 'unrepresentable' senses, such as touch, smell, and taste" (xvi). She states: "When verbal and visual representation is saturated, meanings seep into bodily and other dense, seemingly silent registers" (5). In the absence of visual and auditory clues, the viewers construct Norma through the silent registers of smell as they enter her room.

For the first time, the space of the house and the motel are merged through Norma's voice as part of spatial alignment in the film.

By deliberately refusing to acclimatize the tenor and volume of Norma's voice by the spatial specifics of the film, Hitchcock urges the viewers to carry out their investigation, this time, with their auditory senses. The voice, actually an amalgamation of "three different voices" (Durgnat 2002, 14), has a floating quality that is not rooted in space. Even the shadow of Norma is not properly stabilized in space as Marion, Arbogast, and the viewer see a shadow either framed on a dormer window or floating around with an eerie light in the background thereby arousing the curiosity of both on-screen characters and the viewer. It is the ephemerality of Norma's anatomy on screen that drives the viewers toward discovering this enigmatic character which may perhaps be compared to the interest that incomplete parts of enigmatic animals aroused in viewers—they opened up avenues of uncontrolled imagination and desire and, consequently, the "whole" emerged out of "parts."

Psycho and Nineteenth-Century Miniatures and "Doll Houses"

Polly Morgan in her foreword to Jane Eastoe's *The Art of Taxidermy* (2012) defends contemporary taxidermy by stressing that the art should be seen and appreciated as objectively as possible. If the body acquired is a body that has lived its full course on earth, she states, "[t]o worry about what becomes of the remaining flesh and bone is to foist human codes onto a kingdom that frequently eats its own dead" (Morgan in Eastoe's *The Art of Taxidermy* 2012, Loc. 63 of 1132). Indeed, humans have usually "foisted" their own "codes" on most of the things they encounter. As John Berger, while explaining the age-old human tendency of burdening nonhumans with meanings that pertain to the human world, states, "animals have become prisoners of the human/social situation into which they have been pressganged" (*About Looking* 2009, 19).

By the eighteenth century, with improvements in methods of preservation, complete animal displays were created and relished as sites of subjective investment. It was easier to "foist" our "codes" on bodies that were whole.

Incomplete body parts which were a rage in the sixteenth and seventeenth centuries ceased to fuel the popular imagination. The British Museum which opened in 1753 became home to Hans Sloane's huge collection of curiosities (19,290 specimens of animal parts, according to Melissa Milgrom 2010, 73). But gradually such collections became obsolete and were even regarded as flatly grotesque by the end of the century and were substituted by natural specimens. There was a clear shift in aesthetic indexes as taxidermized re-creations of the eighteenth century did away with offcut miscellanies of the animal body and concentrated on complete mounts. Artists strove for a dramatic rendering of the mood and carriage of the once-alive creatures. Eighteenth-century taxidermy, in keeping with the spirit of the age and its emphasis on symmetry and proportion as yardsticks of beauty, promoted exhibits that were harmonious with contemporary aesthetic principles. Disjointed parts of animal anatomy no longer appealed to contemporary taste. Uniformity and wholeness were the order of the day.

The onset of the Industrial Revolution and a consequent disjunction of humans from the natural world led nineteenth-century England more fervently toward amassing, reviewing, and appreciating specimens from nature. Rachel Poliquin records: "by the mid-nineteenth century taxidermy had reached its apotheosis in Western Europe, and most particularly in England" (2012, 66). She informs: "Taxidermy was everywhere, from the conservatories of the wealthiest patrons to the market stalls, and everywhere in between" (2012, 67). It was, at that time, seen as a marker for reverence of nature and devotion to living beings. Hermann Ploucquet's (1816–78) anti-naturalistic tableaus, Walter Potter's (1835–1918) anthropomorphic museum of curiosities, and Charles Waterton's (1782–1865) use of taxidermy as a trenchant attack on contemporary politics that flourished during the nineteenth century may be read as paradoxical fulfilment of this "return to Nature."

In many such exhibitions, animals that were supposed to bring us close to nature were ironically coerced into the world of humans. The re-creations were made to "ape" human actions as "refashioned" animals were dressed as humans and were displayed as participating in myths and folklore that belonged to the domain of human narratives. Michelle Henning in *Anthropomorphic*

Taxidermy and the Death of Nature: The Curious Art of Hermann Ploucquet, Walter Potter, and Charles Waterton (2007), writes:

> anthropomorphism became a means for nineteenth-century popular displays to negotiate the problematic relationship between people and animals for a thrill-seeking audience. They shared with the curiosity cabinets of the sixteenth and seventeenth centuries a fascination with the anomalous, the hybrid, and the grotesque.
>
> (673)

"[T]he anomalous, the hybrid, and the grotesque" are how we may describe Norma Bates. When Lila and the viewers confront Norma for the first time, silence prevails, pierced a moment later by Lila's scream as she discovers the body of the long-dead woman "dressed in a high-neck, clean, well-pressed dress ... recently laundered and hand-ironed" (Stefano 1959). The taxidermized woman clothed in a "high-neck," "clean," and "hand-ironed" dress is made to participate in a narrative of a thief, a private eye, and a murderer, just as Reynard the Fox is made to playact our childhood fable and dead rabbits are sent to grammar schools and tea parties.

The glass-enclosed curiosity cabinets, on the other hand, find a metaphoric parallel in the Bates house. Hitchcock describes the architectural style of the Bates mansion as "California Gothic" (*Hitchcock/Truffaut* 1984, 269). Rebello describes the architectural design of the Bates world in the following way: "the former like a skeletal finger pointing skyward, the latter a rangy horizontal—on a hill off 'Laramie' street" (1990, 68). Both Stephen Rebello in *The Making of Psycho* (1990) and Steven Jacobs in *The Wrong House* (2013) trace Edward Hopper's 1925 painting *House by the Railroad* as a direct inspiration behind the external structure as well as the basic mood of the house: "from its garret-story, roof-cresting and oculus window, to its cornices and pilasters." Rebello warns, "One might almost expect to glimpse Mrs. Bates silhouetted in the window of the sloping dormer in Hopper's 1925 painting" (1990, 69). The house and Norman's mother may seem grotesque to the viewer, but for Norman, they protect his idyllic past.

The Bates Motel and the Bates House, situated alongside a highway between Phoenix and California, are casualties of road realignments in the fast-emerging 1950s American landscape. The Bates house is a dilapidated mansion brooding over the entire landscape. The Bates Motel, on the other hand, is a product of urbanization and present-day road culture ("One Grey Wall and One Grey Tower," Mondal 2019b, 128). Both the motel and the house, as victims of the spatial arrangement of contemporary commercial development, are cut off from the mainstream because of the construction of a highway that bypasses the Bates motel and mansion. Norman struggles hard to keep this created uncontaminable space intact: "This place … this place happens to be my only world. I grew up in that house up there. I had a very happy childhood. My mother and I were more than happy." This is how he describes his childhood to Sam Loomis (John Gavin). His house to him is a frozen version of a preindustrial world, reminding us of Walton Hall[4] and Walter Potter's tableau: "The enclosed world of the tableau invites nostalgia because of the association of miniaturization with childhood, and with a private temporality which is outside time, along with the delicate handiwork of a pre-industrial world" (Henning 2007, 671). Potter's miniature world is not in contrast to, but rather in tune with, Norman's house. Like Potter's world of miniature creatures that evoke a pre-industrial past with an eye to small details as contrary to the mass production of an industrial state, Norman's house is an extremely subjective idyllic space, carefully constructed and meticulously preserved, where he can escape into an arrested nostalgia by entering his childhood days.

Susan Stewart in *On Longing* focuses on nostalgia while speaking of miniatures: "We cannot separate the function of the miniature from a nostalgia for pre-industrial labor, a nostalgia for craft" (1993, 68). She sees miniature

---

[4] As Waterton grew more and more wary of the people around, he built a three-mile long and a sixteen-feet high wall around his property, Walton Hall in Wakefield at Yorkshire, England, to keep people away. Blackburn explains, "[t]he wall had a … more diffuse symbolic purpose. It was as if Waterton felt that once he has enclosed his huge garden, he might be able to control his own restlessness, and to provide himself with a place where he felt at ease … The park, with its tall trees and its gentle creatures, was to be a peaceable kingdom, an earthly paradise where there was no need to learn fear … It was to have the sense of security which he had known as a child; magically kept just out of reach of the growing horrors of the modern world" (1991, 112). Here, the taxidermists Norman Bates and Charles Waterton, creators of outrageous specimens, come together as loners, as ones attempting to keep their childhood memories and associations alive. Both the real Waterton and the fictional Bates were acutely conscious of their familiar world crumbling around them. Their conserved properties are testaments of a visual allegory that resists the crushing impact of modernization and their preserved specimens serve as archives of irreversible losses.

products as a reaction against mass production. Against cheap readily available market products that can easily be replicated and reproduced en masse, the miniatures stand for an antithetical aesthetics—hand-made and exclusive, they snub at cheap repetitions (Stewart 1993, 68). Taxidermy, dealing with the skin of a once-alive body is an art that requires careful manipulation, skill, and patience. It is unique not only for the exotic/exclusive raw material used but also for its painstaking practitioner who forges new bodies out of old ones, and sometimes, as in the case of Norman, searches old bodies in newly forged ones. His tableau and his art may be grotesque, but they carry his distinctive mark.

Norma's Doll's House

Norma Bates' room, preserved by Norman, within the Bates mansion has the quality of an untouched dollhouse:

> A house within a house, the dollhouse not only presents the house's articulation of the tension between inner and outer spheres, of exteriority and interiority—it also represents the tension between two modes of interiority. Occupying a space within an enclosed space … The dollhouse is a materialized secret; what we look for is the dollhouse within the dollhouse and its promise of an infinitely profound interiority.
>
> (Stewart, quoted by Henning 2007, 61)

In sharp contrast to the utilitarian bare-bone feel of the Bates Motel rooms, the packed surface of the Bates House pronounces a sense of temporal and spatial incarceration. It gives us a feeling of extravagance and the impression of a hermetically sealed world. Susan Stewart, perhaps speaks of such a supposedly "pure" ossified space that a miniature dollhouse brings forth, "The miniature world remains perfect and uncontaminated by the grotesque so long as its absolute boundaries are maintained" (1993, 68).

Preservation of memory through corporeality is what Norman practices and preservation of an idyllic space sealed off from the outside world is what he struggles to protect. Like Potter and Waterton, and their preoccupation with a world fading fast under the impact of rapid industrialization, Norman tries to retain some vestige of the old-world order already crumbling under the weight of highways and fancy motels and the pursuit of the American Dream. It is a dilapidated mansion that he chooses as his diorama, a Victorian room as his tableau, and a dead mother as his specimen. The gigantic dollhouse that Norman creates for himself, though huge in dimension compared to a miniature dollhouse, has all the features of a carefully contained neat border of a dollhouse, a space within a space where time is illusory. This space can never be invaded by an onlooker. Like the glass-encased exhibits of Potter, it remains a forbidden world for outsiders. Just as one can only see and never participate in the world of a dollhouse, one can have glimpses of a window and the silhouette of an old woman without the possibility of venturing within. A flouting of that privacy and an attempt at tampering with that space predictably proves fatal.

As Stewart warns, this insular space can be spoilt easily if its "absolute boundaries" are violated. We, along with Lila, disregard the "boundaries" and face the consequence. Bernard Herrmann's music and the camera movement forebode the consequence. They predict entrapment and enclosure. The forward tracking point-of-view shots of Lila getting closer to the house create almost an ominous sense of the entire structure of the house advancing as well to overwhelm her. Jack Sullivan in *Hitchcock's Music* (2006) states: "Everywhere the music suggests enclosure. The grim figures in contrary motion during 'The Hill' draw Lila toward the house we desperately want her to not enter, the violins sliding down as the basses creep up—a brilliant evocation of entrapment" (257). As we journey with Lila into the Bates House to know the secret of Norma's room, we discover that this meticulously arranged room is protected by a forbidding entrance and an imposing stairway. Lila's investigating the layered space of the Bates House seems like a never-ending narrative of "a house within a house" with their ever-increasing grim depths. Lila crosses the portico that leads to the stairway that in turn leads to Norma's room and then she enters Norman's room and then again into the basement. What the viewers are greeted with is a perpetually deepening interiority. Lila and the viewers seem sucked into this petrifying space where there is no room for outsiders, no room for a complacent viewing. Unlike the visitors of Potter's Museum, we become participants who enter the recesses of a dangerous tableau. The room with an absent mother's indent on the bed leads to the further pits of a basement that in turn leads to a dead body again leading to an emptiness within her. Thus, a penetration of the depths of an interior that does not seem to end reminds us of Stewart's "dollhouse and its promise of an infinitely profound interiority."

Norman guards his tableau and his art ferociously and would easily go to the extent of killing anyone who dares to enter his mother's room, a repository where he has meticulously mummified his shared bygone days with her. He will not allow the present to contaminate this space of his created past. This space is threatened by two intruders: detective Milton Arbogast and Marion's sister, Lila Crane. On both occasions the results are catastrophic. Arbogast is killed and Lila is almost killed. Taxidermists, easily invading the space of the body, loathe invasion of their workspace. In *Still Life* (2010) Melissa Milgrom speaks of the blinkeredness of the taxidermists in their reluctance in sharing their secret recipes:

> taxidermists, who tend to be solitary workers, purposely cut themselves off from the outside world. No other profession has so steadfastly barred visitors from its dreary workshops ... Gruesome dissections took place in dark, smelly rooms ... Arsenic, formalin, carbon tetrachloride, and other dangerous chemicals that taxidermists used as preservatives were stored in open containers and filled the workshops' stagnant air with carcinogenic dust.
>
> (2010, 14)

Norman's house is a dystopic studio where the living and the dead merge. The Bates house may be seen both as the workshop and as the diorama of Norman—a refuge, a dream, and yet a source of terror as it is also a space that conceals the shock of matricide. Unlike a miniature world of perfect corpses, Norman's mother at times becomes a grotesque specimen even to her creator. Ironically the house is both a "refuge" that Norman clings to, and yet a dystopic space from which he wants to "claw" his way out. The motel consequently is transformed into a temporary shelter for a son tortured and tormented by the memories of a mother he had killed. It is only when his created specimen comes out to ravage and kill in a space consigned to visitors that we feel the menace and the fluidity of the two seemingly opposing spatial boundaries, making it apparent that Norman has no place to "claw" out of. It is neither the house nor the motel that has confined him. It is his body that has become a space of his asphyxiation. It is his body that is his workshop, his diorama, his dollhouse, and his nightmare.

Norman's room with its tattered toys, a cramped tiny bed, Beethoven's Eroica, a gramophone, and hard-bound nameless books carry, like his mother's room, the unmistakable marks of time held in confinement. The architecture of the Bates house reminds us of Chris Baldick's definition of the Gothic in *The Oxford Book of Gothic Tales* (2001):

> For the Gothic effect to be attained, a tale should combine a fearful sense of inheritance in time with a claustrophobic sense of enclosure in space, these two dimensions reinforcing one another to produce an impression of sickening descent into disintegration.
>
> (xix)

It is through this claustrophobic confinement in ill-aired spaces that we experience, along with the characters on-screen, the "sickening descent into disintegration," not unlike an airless glass-encased world of dead kittens, dead rabbits, and dead birds. Like Potter forging his kittens and birds, Ploucquet creating his Reynard, and Waterton walling up his Walton Hall, Norman's refashioning his mother's corpse and preserving his Victorian mansion, are attempts to ward off the onslaught of a dystopic present and preserve his private distorted dollhouse.

Fin de siècle habitat diorama

The glass-enclosed worlds of miniature exhibits and anthropomorphic displays gave way to habitat dioramas at the turn of the century. The end of the nineteenth century and the first half of the twentieth century saw Americans leading in field expeditions for the acquiring of unknown animals from distant continents like Africa, Asia, and Australia. Voyagers, nature enthusiasts, and taxidermists were sponsored to undertake journeys to collect specimens for museums as well as for scientific investigations. The American Museum of Natural History sent more than a thousand expeditions. China,

Australia, and Papua New Guinea had become rich fields for zoological surveys and specimen acquisitions (Milgrom 2010, 75–6). According to Milgrom's record, "about two thousand mammals and mammal skeletons, eight hundred birds, and two hundred reptiles" (Milgrom 2010, 76) were killed in a single expedition to South China led by Roy Chapman Andrews. The only explanation for such a staggering amount of destruction was that two-thirds of the species accrued had never been seen in America before. Fascination and curiosity toward a creation, merged with an urge to possess it, proves fatal for the desired object.

We may cite Carl Ethan Akeley's obsession with African wilderness as a case in point. Carl Ethan Akeley (1864–1926), the legendary *fin de siècle* taxidermist, revolutionized the art of taxidermy by elevating it from a crude stuffing of animal carcasses to the level of sculpture. His habitat dioramas in the American Museum of Natural History and the Field Museum in Chicago have raised taxidermy to a new height where the grotesque has no place. Milgrom defines a diorama as "three-dimensional time capsules of vanishing landscapes. Like meticulous stage sets, they simulate reality with dreamlike precision. Dioramas depict places in the world that are no longer as beautiful or as 'natural' as they used to be" (2010: 26). The different species are well separated and every animal or bird is shown in its natural habitat—artificially created—with no human interference in the scene. It is the life-likeness of an animal that was a trademark of an Akeley mount. Milgrom quotes paleontologist Roy Chapman Andrews: "If you want to see a live elephant, you can go to a circus or a zoo. But if you want to see the way an elephant lives, you go to a good museum of natural history. And you owe much of what you see there to the genius of Carl Akeley" (2010, 70). Akeley was sent on several expeditions by the American Museum of Natural History to Africa. He spent his entire career reproducing "every twig," "every grain of sand," and "every star in the sky" of the African wilderness in America (Milgrom 2010, 70). However, this does not ease our discomfort regarding the mounts as the very art rests on the conflating of life and death. The skin looks life-like, but beneath the skin scuttles the emptiness of the dead. Moreover, the obsession of Akeley to recreate Africa in America may be read, in Donna Haraway's vein, as a white man's desire to tame and sanitize the wilderness of Africa by killing and then preserving the dead bodies of its wild animals in neatly cloistered compartments.

Akeley was enamored by the ephemerality of the beauty of the African flora and fauna. Such naturalists could overlook the gruesome act of killing, ignore the violence that necessarily accompanies such acts of re-composition, and bathe in the sheer pleasure of re-created natural beauty, thus rendered unnatural. Basking in the borrowed beauty of animals that their homeland could not produce, these creators brought home specimens that would have otherwise remained unknown to contemporary nature lovers. This, ironically, remains the only excuse for their acts of rummaging through the outside world and systematically exploiting it to create at home a simulacrum of an exotic natural abode with coveted species as hard-earned trophies.

When one is devoted to something intensely, one tends to preserve and possess it, but if one wants to preserve and possess it permanently, and that too in an unchanged form, one first has to destroy it. It is perhaps out of this dilemma that taxidermy was born. Carl Ethan Akeley's passion for reconstructing not merely a replica of any animal, but rather a recreation of one particular animal, *his* animal, *his* creation sets him apart from other minor taxidermists. Mary Jobe Akeley in *The Wilderness Lives Again* (1940) describes in graphic detail the process of killing, skinning, tanning, and preserving animals practiced by her husband, Carl. Her description of Akeley recreating an elephant shows the skill and dexterity of a man simulating nature with a fidelity that verges on madness:

> Properly skinning an animal is incredibly difficult, particularly in primitive conditions. Akeley skinned animals like a Park Avenue plastic surgeon. All his incisions minimized future seams, so they'd disappear when the animal was assembled later. The legs were cut on the inside; the back was cut longitudinally along the spine; the head was cast, cut off. Once skinned, the elephant was fleshed, a far more grueling task. It took Akeley and his team of porters four to five days to remove and prepare the thick, two thousand pound hide, using small knives so that they would not mar the skin. When the salted skin arrived in the museum workshop, it was hard and stiff and had to be tanned—a twelve-week process of daily turning to achieve optimum suppleness. (Mary Jobe Akeley said that her husband's tanning

formula ... was so good that he never lost a wrinkle, a wart, or a tick hole.) Eventually, the two—and a—half-inch- thick hide was reduced to a quarter inch leather (soft as a glove) and was ready for mounting.

(quoted by Milgrom 2010, 81)

Such works of precision had to have a strong impression on the beholders. Carl Akeley, while twisting, turning, and manipulating the animal could also have envisaged the reactions of the visitors who would come to visit his dream project—a diorama of Africa in the United States, a diorama so perfect that one would be transported back in time and space to the wilderness of the "heart of darkness."

Past sixty, lying on a stretcher, a few days before his death in the lush rain forest of what was then the Belgian Congo, Carl Akeley tells his wife: "Mary, this is the Kivu at last. Here the fairies play! Isn't this forest the most beautiful, the most ancient in all the world?" (Milgrom 2010, 84). It is this "beautiful," this "ancient" world that he had tried to reproduce in New York and for which he had devoted more than twenty years of his life. He did not live to see the completion of his dream diorama, the African Hall. But he died loving the forests of Africa, its flora and fauna. Yet to replicate them he had to destroy them first. In the process, he perhaps destroyed himself as well. Both Akeley and Hitchcock's Norman lose themselves in their dioramas; it is in Norman's house that his "fairies play!"

Ethics and Aesthetics of Modern Taxidermy

The aesthetic and ethical aspects of taxidermy have usually been tied up in a complex problematic relationship: a problem that became more pronounced during the second half of the twentieth and the early twenty-first centuries. The nineteenth- and early twentieth-century fascination for nature meant its destruction, while a mid-twentieth-century love of nature was usually accompanied by serious concerns about its conservation. Attachment to natural species entailed feeling, and not possessing, the coveted creatures. The trend was more toward a preference for the fleeting experience of coming into contact with real nature and real animals and not the fixed static posture of a frigid mount reminding us of our systematic well-planned cruelty.

From the mid-twentieth century to the present day the responses toward taxidermy have varied widely and intensely. The brevity of a real experience or the complacent viewing of exotica on-screen is pitted against the uneasy, yet exciting, sensations of a prolonged encounter with a manhandled re-creation on display. Victorian appreciation of dead exhibits is in sharp contrast to a present-day re-evaluation of taxidermy precisely because the cultural connotations associated with the beauty or dread of an animal have altered. Unprecedented technological advancements that bring documentaries and video footage of distant exotic creatures within the familiar precincts of our homes are largely responsible for such changes in attitudes to the art of taxidermy. Viewing exotic animals no longer remains an uphill task. Destroying an animal to appreciate its beauty for an extensive period seems an absurd idea today.

Concern for animal rights, wildlife preservation laws,[5] and a clear shift in the cultural response to taxidermy had already begun to see the art as the grotesque mind's propensity to create grotesque bodies. Taxidermy, for the next few decades, was relegated to the margins, only to be revived in the late 1960s when taxidermy again found its foothold in the realm of popular culture. Taxidermy schools and associations proliferated. Trade magazines sponsoring and arranging international competitions of animal displays became frequent. Taxidermy became once more a favorite for ones with a taste for natural beauty with a generous slathering of the morbid. Present-day taxidermists, however, use roadkill, contributions from owners of pets and veterinarians, and unused animal remnants from museums and academic centers to practice their art.

Surprisingly, taxidermy was brought forth in mainstream cinema by Hitchcock during a phase when it was at a lower ebb of its popularity as an art. The first mainstream Hitchcock film that employs this art concretely but fleetingly is *The Man Who Knew Too Much* made in 1956. As a departure

---

[5] Jane Eastoe, in *The Art of Taxidermy*, for instance, mentions the Convention on International Trade in Endangered Species of Wild Fauna and Flora (CITES) legislation, an agreement between nations to safeguard the lives of animals and plants. Taxidermists, post-1947, are compelled to abide by the rules of the CITES legislation regarding ownership of species, both alive and dead (2012, Loc. 95 of 1132. Kindle).

from the 1934 original version, Benjamin McKenna (James Stewart) in the 1956 remake, in search of his kidnapped son, is misled into the taxidermy shop of "Ambrose Chappell." Unlike Hitchcock's usual practice of shooting in a studio this was a location shooting and the setting was the real taxidermy shop of Edward Gerrard and Sons at 61 Burdett Street in London. The taxidermy shop sequence is a hilarious piece where McKenna's interaction with the taxidermist, Ambrose Chappell, their speaking at cross purposes, and the scuffle that ensues which ultimately leads to McKenna's hand getting stuck within the jaws of a snarling tiger, all provoke mirth in an otherwise tense chase-drama. However, Hitchcock's comic reliefs are usually in tune with the macabre potentials of his films. The scene begins with an ominous tone as McKenna enters the narrow alley that leads to the taxidermy workshop. Forward tracking point-of-view shots of McKenna are meticulously balanced by counter shots of the London alley walls coming forward to overpower him. This series of camera movements prophesy an exact sequence of camera movements four years later when Lila enters the mad world of the Bates mansion in *Psycho*. Music—the slow consistent mounting of chords punctuated by the sound of church bells—evokes a sense of foreboding, apprehending again the music of *Psycho* at the moment of Lila's opening the main door of the Bates portico. What McKenna finds inside the building he enters is not much different from what Lila finds in the Bates House—taxidermized specimens. Both McKenna and Lila have gone in pursuit of someone they love dearly. And both their pursuits fail. The difference is, while inside, McKenna's hands get trapped within the jaws of a dead tiger, and Lila gets trapped by the empty eye sockets of the dead Mother. McKenna's misadventure makes us laugh, and Lila's venturing into the forbidden basement makes us shriek. The reforged dead specimens that clutter Chappell's workshop are, therefore, uneasy teasers of what Hitchcock had in store for us—a reforged dead Mother.

The art of taxidermy as part of macabre humor addressed in *The Man Who Knew Too Much* (1956) becomes a more intriguing discourse in *Psycho*. Taxidermy contains the crux of the mystery in the film. Incidentally, post *Psycho*, America witnessed a revival of interest in taxidermy. Whether *Psycho* (1960), the novel on which the film is based (Robert Bloch's *Psycho*, 1959), and the real story of Ed Gein (on which Bloch's novel is based) were, in some morbid way, instrumental in reviving interest in this almost-dead art is debatable. But the acute interest stirred by the news of the body parts and skin found in the Wisconsin murders,[6] the immense popularity of Bloch's body horror *Psycho* and the huge success of Hitchcock's thriller *Psycho* shed light on contemporary viewer's/reader's craving for the sensational and the corporeal. *Psycho* perhaps may have fueled the viewers' curiosity about re-created macabre bodies. The popularity of *Psycho* and the series of slasher films (that fed on female flesh) it spawned brought to the fore that contemporary interest in corporeality was reviving. Or perhaps the interest was always there and *Psycho* had simply removed the skin of genteel restraint.

A Rogue Taxidermist and His Dreary Workshop

Twenty-first-century scholars who work on taxidermy take pains in revisiting Victorian exhibits to eke cultural, social, and political meanings out of them. While Michelle Henning visits the miniature glass cases of Ploucquet, Potter, and Waterton, Bryndís Snæbjörnsdóttir and Mark Wilson search for mounted polar bears amid household debris, roadside pubs, and natural history museums in the UK. Melissa Milgrom, on the other hand, visits her neighboring taxidermy workshop—Schwendeman's Taxidermy Studio—at Milltown, New Jersey. She describes "Schwendeman's" as "a motionless zoo" (2010, 2): "Roughly one thousand dusty-eyed birds and exotic stuffed

---

[6] Joseph Smith in *The Psycho Files: A Comprehensive Guide to Hitchcock's Classic Shocker* reports: "During the days and weeks following the gruesome discoveries in Ed Gein's home, police stood guard on the house around the clock 'to discourage curiosity seekers, including groups of fraternity boys from the University of Wisconsin bent on throwing beer parties in the infamous "house of horror."' Carloads of rubber-neckers poured through the town—perhaps as many as 4,000 families just on the Sunday following Gein's arrest. A few months later, a crowd of 20,000 descended on Plainfield when Gein's property was opened to the public before its sale by auction. But by then, there wasn't much to see; only three days earlier, the Gein house had burned to the ground, probably torched by local residents irritated over the hordes of gawkers—and by their town's sullied reputation" (2009, 11).

beasts roost on the countertops and hang from the ceiling and walls. It's so cluttered with mounted animals (and skeletons and strange tools) that no one's ever bothered to take an inventory" (2010, 2). In stark contrast to Milgrom's description of Schwendeman's Studio stands the art space of Snæbjörnsdóttir and Wilson titled "Nanoq—Flat Out and Bluesome" where ten polar bears, brought together from different parts of the UK, stand in solitary glass cases—a huge austere display space that is "marked by a sense of absence, an uneasy silence, a loneliness, and longing … with its white walls, white floor, glass, clean white metal, and isolated honey-white bears" (Poliquin 2012, 2).

Art spaces, curiosity cabinets, museums, habitat dioramas, studios, workshops, roadside inns, and drawing room parlors—spaces that house taxidermy exhibits may be as varied and as contrasting as the exhibits and our reading of and reactions to them. The spatial composition of *Psycho* is such that it accommodates everything—a melting pot that can easily be related to the loneliness of the ten white bears in the "Nanoq" project, the queasiness of witnessing the debulking of a heron at Schwendeman's, the nostalgia for a lost past in a Potter or a Ploucquet cabinet. The Bates world connotes macabre curiosity, seediness, horror, fascination, and above all, longing.

Ken Roy Walker expresses himself to Milgrom: "You can almost hear a heart beat. You can almost see the spark of life, and it's a gift to bring the spark of life back" (Milgrom 2010, 41). On the other hand, Jack Fishwick has an opposite take on the art of taxidermy—"Even though I do it, I think it is totally weird. Bizarre! It's a pointless exercise, because it will never be perfect. No matter how good you are, you'll only get a semblance of life. It'll never be alive again" (Milgrom 2010, 52). A group of contemporary taxidermists has a third approach to the art. Doing away with the graver aspects and concerns of taxidermy, we have a section of taxidermists who term themselves "Rogue Taxidermists." Much in the vein of nineteenth-century taxidermists, like Ploucquet, Potter, and Waterton, the rogue taxidermists create freak specimens of nonhumans engaged in highly eccentric human gestures. They call their art "crap taxidermy" as they rearrange taxidermized animals in outright freakish tableaus with each body as a grotesque montage:

> Fast-forward to the early 2000s, and taxidermy took a bold step into the absurd with the Rogue Taxidermy movement. Stuffed animals started to appear in fashionable New York art galleries. This new generation of artists thought nothing of messing with nature, combining body parts to create flying goat-fish creatures or three-headed mice.
>
> (*Taxidermy Gone Wrong* by Rob Colson 2020, 2)

Rob Colson's *Taxidermy Gone Wrong* (2020) is a fascinating and yet macabre volume that brings together card-playing toads, bike-riding gun-toting squirrels, book-reading coffee-drinking porcupines, biscuit-stealing rats, love-struck gophers, mourning crows, murderous mice and many more reminding us of Ploucquet, Potter and Waterton's unusual Victorian menageries. These twenty-first-century anthropomorphic displays reproduced on the pages of a single volume are both an acceptance of the absurdity inherent in the very art of taxidermy and a celebration of human creativity. It even depicts our ability to laugh at ourselves.

Much to his dismay, Norman may be called a "rogue taxidermist" and his Mother could well be an instance of "crap taxidermy" as she is uncannily akin

Figure 2.1 Norma Bates in the basement, *Psycho*.

to a popular exhibit of freak side shows—the "Fiji Mermaid." A Mermaid—an archetypal mythical figure in the shared imaginary of the human world for centuries—is created by combining the head of a monkey and the tail of a fish, a "Re-Creation" again.[7]

The preserved Norma is described by Stefano in the following words:

> It is the body of a woman long dead. The skin is dry and pulled away from the mouth and the teeth are revealed as in the skeleton's smile. The eyes are gone from their sockets, the bridge of the nose has collapsed, the hair is dry and wild, the cheeks are sunken, the leathery-brown skin is powdered and rouged and flaky.
>
> (Stefano 1959)

Rob Colson's *Taxidermy Gone Wrong* (2020) includes Cory Doctorow's Fiji Mermaid (99) which looks exactly like Norma Bates. Doctorow's Mermaid is an old, disheveled woman with the body and scales of a fish and the head of a monkey. Norman, who could meticulously preserve birds (as is evident on his parlor walls), could not preserve his mother well. She is decrepit, old, well into her path of decay, and could easily be employed as "a freak show staple" like the Fiji Mermaid of Doctorow. Her slowly decaying skin (leathery-brown and parched is how the script describes it), is a sad testament to the slow erosion of the dead and a cruel reminder of the futility of preservation. She is not the kind of "bird" Norman wanted her to be. He can never make his mother live again. His mother is merely a warped remake of a mad son, a perverse reminder of "what was" but "never shall be." It is this refusal to come to terms with the unmistakable deadness of a body and the futility of trying to reproduce a perfect body that Norman carries within him so much so that his body becomes a kind of diorama where mother and son, submission and struggle, and loathing and love blend.[8] Again, it is not only Norman whose body is a

---

[7] See Peabody Museum: Archaeology and Ethnology, "FeeJee Mermaid." https://www.youtube.com/watch?v=C1g7QbP4rM4 for a detailed description of a Fiji Mermaid, a Re-Creation, popularized by P. T. Barnum in 1842, a combination of a spider monkey and a fish with "reptile claws ... papier mâché" and "clay woolly bits" (Peabody Museum: "FeeJee Mermaid," 2:04).

[8] The psychiatrist toward the end explains: "He stole her corpse... and a weighted coffin was buried. He hid the body in the fruit cellar, even 'treated' it to keep it as well as it would keep. And that still wasn't enough. She was there, but she was a corpse. So, he began to think and speak for her, gave her half his life, so to speak" (*Psycho* 1960).

melting pot of opposites. The wasted shell of Norma Bates is a repository of juxtapositions. The "body" of Norma becomes a surrogate home for Norman. It is a tableau where Norman becomes a specimen. He is that taxidermist who becomes a pathetic exhibit of his dystopic diorama, a grotesque product of his workshop.

3

Illusory Souvenirs: Memory, Beauty, and Hitchcock's Women in *Psycho*, *Vertigo*, *The Birds*, and *Marnie*

"What if diamonds become the new urn?" asks Adelle Archer, the co-founder and CEO of Eterneva (Natsuki 2022, 6:36). Eterneva is a radical death care company that creates memorial diamonds from the carbon found in the ashes of the dead. At a price ranging from 2,999 dollars to 50,000 dollars, Eterneva, and a few other death care companies, convert the ashes of humans and pets into diamonds.[1] Likewise, "The Death Scent Project"[2] claims a successful extraction of odor molecules from a deceased's material remnants and their preservation as perfumes. The twenty-first century has invested a lot into grief research and has already opened newer avenues to preserve the corporeal memory of the one who departs for the one who remains. The smell, the hair, and the ashes from the bones of a body are conserved as tokenistic substitutes for the departed one. From embalming and mummification of ancient times to the contemporary practice of converting loved ones' ashes into jewelry and conserving the scent of a loved one in a perfume bottle, these are all parts of a continuous attempt to preserve memories. We are petrified of changes; we are bad at letting things go. The industry of mourning technology thrives today on this primal human need. However, unlike the art of taxidermy, the preservation work done by the death care companies does not entail force or violence. Besides a certain longing for a body, it is this violence, this obsession

---

[1] See https://eterneva.com/memorial-diamond-cost/
[2] See https://deathscent.com/2016/10/12/oct-5th-bottling-ghosts-can-should-we-try-to-capture-the-scent-of-our-dead-loved-ones/

to control a body completely, to make it perform or pose in a way that the creator deems fit, that makes taxidermy as a method of preservation different from other methods of preservation.

"I Have to Go Back into the Past Once More"

Although taxidermized bodies appear in Alfred Hitchcock's *Psycho* and *The Man Who Knew Too Much* (1956), the motif of a remade body runs through many of Hitchcock's films. In *Rebecca* (1940), Mrs. De Winter struggles to fit in the absent body of Rebecca; Barbara Morton serves as a visual re-embodiment of Miriam Haines in *Strangers on a Train* (1951); *The Wrong Man* (1956) toys with the dangers of a look-alike; *Vertigo* (1958) again is a film where borrowed memories seek refuge in borrowed bodies.

Memory plays a key role in Alfred Hitchcock's films, especially during his American phase. *Rebecca* (1940), his first film in America, centers around a protagonist who is absent throughout the film. The material remnants of the potently present yet absent Rebecca propel the plot forward and become the source of crisis in the lives of the De Winters (Laurence Olivier and Joan Fontaine) and Mrs. Danvers (Judith Anderson). Hitchcock does not present Rebecca on-screen. She is dead from the very beginning of the film. The viewers can only visualize her (like Norma in *Psycho*) through her robes, toiletries, mirror, bed, and the elaborate ravings of Mrs. Danvers who worships her. Hitchcock creates a *mise-en-scène* in our shared imagination where Rebecca becomes much more prominent than the very present Mrs. De Winter who replaces Rebecca in the De Winter household. Manderley is filled with memories of Rebecca so much so that the living Mrs. De Winter seems like a shadow lurking at the corners of the vast rooms where Rebecca ruled. Memory is usually a recollection of something we have seen or experienced. *Rebecca* brings forth another dimension of memory: the memory of something that we have never seen before, the memory of absence, the memory of a void filled in by an imagined body.

Like *Rebecca* and *Psycho*, *Vertigo* too engages with memory that manifests itself through the body of a woman. In *Vertigo*, Hitchcock explores the memory of an illusory body, bringing once again, the art of taxidermy to mind. Scottie (James Stewart) metaphorically acts like a taxidermist. He takes the skin of Judy Barton (Kim Novak) and stretches it to fit the manikin of Madeleine Elster. The entire film centers on a constant search for one person in another person's body. Scottie Ferguson relentlessly and obsessively tracks a woman's transformation—from Carlotta Valdes to Madeleine Elster to Judy Barton—while attempting to come to terms with his inner devils, his acrophobia, and vertigo. *Vertigo* metaphorically brings out a fascinating but poignant feature of taxidermy. It focuses on how an actual body becomes a stage where the re-enactment of an imagined body takes place. The body no longer remains a mere tool for performance; the body itself becomes a performance of memory, a locus where the past is recreated. Hitchcock's *Vertigo* is a film about lent bodies, a film where past and present; fantasies and nightmares, the real and the imaginary commingle to make the film a repository of myriad memories. Scottie Ferguson's refusal to come out of his reminiscences of Madeleine Elster, his constant efforts to recreate Madeleine in Judy Barton, and the search for a lost body in the body of another individual, bring forth the idea of the body as a locus with immense possibilities. Just as it is a concrete physical representation of its materiality, it is also a constant reminder of a body that *was* and no longer *is*.

"Let Me Take Care of You, Judy"—Scottie

Taxidermy is both the memory and the quest for a body. *Vertigo* is a tale of these relentless quests. With Scottie Ferguson, we traverse the length and breadth of San Francisco in search of a mysterious woman. The plot of the film runs thus: while trying to recuperate from his near-fatal accident and his acrophobia, Scottie is summoned by his old college friend Gavin Elster (Tom Helmore) to keep a constant vigil on his wife Madeleine Elster. Gavin convinces Scottie that Madeleine is possessed by the spirit of her grandmother Carlotta Valdes who, after being abandoned by her lover and being deprived of her child, had lost her sanity and committed suicide. Scottie follows Madeleine through the streets of San Francisco, through museums, cemeteries, restaurants, and flower shops and one day saves her from committing suicide at the bay near Golden Gate Bridge. They grow closer and Scottie becomes more and more obsessed with Madeleine. To cure Madeleine of the nightmares of her death, Scottie probes and finds out that she dreams of a church tower and takes her to the Bell Tower of the Mission San Juan Bautista. Once there, Madeleine grows restless, and climbs up the church tower and jumps, while Scottie fails to climb up the stairs and save her because of his fear of heights.

The second half of the film shows Scottie roaming about the streets, mistaking other women for Madeleine, until one day he comes across a woman who is remarkably akin to Madeleine. He follows her to her hotel room and the woman reveals that she is Judy Barton from Kansas. Her gait and her demeanor do not resemble Madeleine in the slightest way. Judy is more vibrant. We first see her as a brunette in a bright green dress and flashy make-up. She is an absolute contrast to the blonde Madeleine. Scottie, now completely obsessed with Madeleine, sets upon remaking Judy into Madeleine. He buys her clothes, shoes, and accessories keeping Madeleine in mind. He even forces her to change the color of her hair. Scottie compels Judy to enter the past world that Madeleine inhabited. Her dress and her hair are stripped of the bright colors they possessed, making her as spectral as Madeleine.

It is only when her transformation is complete that Judy wears a necklace that Carlotta Valdes had worn in the portrait, thereby revealing unwittingly to Scottie that Judy and Madeleine were the same person. Madeleine was a creation of Gavin Elster. She had been constructed by Gavin as a substitute for his real wife and it was Gavin's wife who was thrown down the tower, while Scottie paralyzed by his fear rooted at a lower landing of the tower, mistook Elster's wife to be Madeleine, and thereby became a convenient witness who testified that Elster's wife had committed suicide. Thus, the dream that Scottie was pursuing, the dream that he was transforming into reality through Judy's body was Gavin Elster's creation. He was chasing a memory that had been dished out to him by his friend. He was creating a woman who had already been fashioned and tailor-made by another man. Scottie fails to create an obedient female anatomy. Maddened by this failure, Scottie takes Judy to the same site of the previous accident where Judy tries to convince him of her love for him. But they are greeted by another tragedy. Judy seeing the shadow of a nun panics and falls down the tower; and Scottie, finally cured of his vertigo, watches from the edge.

From the very first shot in *Vertigo*, we are escorted into Scottie's perspective. We see most of the incidents unfolding, at least in the first half of the film, through Scottie's eyes. Robin Wood in *Hitchcock's Films Revisited* (2002), elaborates:

> Leisurely, steady-paced subjective tracking shots characterize the sequences in which Scottie follows Madeleine; we are placed behind the windscreen of his car in the driver's seat as he follows her around the streets of San Francisco, pursuing a dream through modern surface reality; we wander at his walking pace round the graveyard; we watch Madeleine continually through his eyes, her distance, her silence, his and our inability to understand her, help her, protect her, are all a part of the fascination.
>
> (114)

Much in the spirit of a Gothic tale, the setting, the characters, and the plot in *Vertigo* revolve around an inability to escape the fetters of the past: cemeteries, museums, the abode of the long-dead Carlotta Valdes, and the entire cityscape of San Francisco seethe with a sense of loss. Madeleine is constantly associated with the past, the dead, the time that was, the body that was: She leads him back always to the past—the grave, the portrait, the house of a long-dead woman—"the fascination she exerts is the fascination of death" (Wood 2002, 114).

The abundant use of point-of-view shots, soft light, and diffusion filters; the recurrence of romantic strains on the soundtrack; the muted hues of the settings in the first half of the film, make us travel with Scottie into a world of memories. With Scottie, we follow Madeleine into the world of Carlotta Valdes, to the Golden Gate Bridge, to the art museum, to the Mission Dolores, and to the McKittrick Hotel. But ironically it is a past that is created by Gavin Elster. The memories that seem to haunt Madeleine are not real; they are construed by a trickster. Further, the viewers identifying themselves with Scottie participate in this tawdry world of make-believe memories. Memory becomes a tool of exploitation that a gullible viewer and an equally gullible protagonist cling to. Scottie falls in love with an image. He becomes obsessed with a woman who never existed.

Here Hitchcock's reading of the plot of *Vertigo* is significant. He says: "To put it plainly, the man wants to go to bed with a woman who is dead; he is indulging in a form of necrophilia." He further elaborates: "Cinematically, all of Stewart's efforts to *recreate* the dead woman are shown in such a way that he seems to be trying to undress her, instead of the other way round" (*Hitchcock/Truffaut* 1984, 244). By identifying with Scottie, we tend to impose the illusory Madeleine on the real Judy, undressing and dressing her in borrowed robes. Madeleine Elster is destroyed to bring in Judy Barton. Once Judy appears on screen, we all try to find traces of Madeleine in her, knowing fully well that she never *was* Madeleine.

"If I Let You Change Me, Will That Do It? … Will You Love Me?"—Judy

Unlike Scottie, Judy falls in love with a real person that Scottie is. But she had been a participant in the creation of a deceptive body. Mainstream narrative cinema, therefore, sets out to punish her for her audacity. She becomes a living embodiment of a body that she had actively created with Elster; an anatomy that stifles her, contains her, and ultimately destroys her. Her body becomes a locus of repeated transformations as she transmutes from Madeleine to Carlotta to Judy to Madeleine again. Her body becomes a site of unending false memories: it becomes the apparition of Carlotta, a body double of Elster's wife, and an object of obsession for Scottie. In the first half of the film, Madeleine is shaped by the memory of Carlotta's body as we see her sitting in front of Carlotta's portrait in the museum. The camera takes a close shot of the bouquet placed beside Madeleine, then tilts up and moves forward to an extreme close shot of the bouquet beside Carlotta in the portrait. This is followed by a close shot of Madeleine's knot of hair and a forward tracking shot of a close-up of Carlotta's similar coiffure. These constant parallel forward tracking shots manage to blur the distinction between a real body and a painted body so much so that Madeleine's body itself becomes a re-embodiment of Carlotta Valdes: a living embodiment of a dead body that was never alive.

In the second movement of the film, the pattern remains the same. Only this time, it is Judy who has to carry the burden of Madeleine's memory in her body. On both occasions, ironically, the men are the real choreographers of the makeover, while the woman remains a mere puppet acting and dressing according to the caprices of the men in her life. As Tania Modleski in *The Women Who Knew Too Much* (2005) states: "the female character, Madeleine/Judy, is like a living doll whom the hero strips and changes and makes over according to his ideal image" (2005, 91). Judy's body is used as a shell that is repeatedly filled, emptied, and refilled by people from the past, people who are dead, or people who are mere constructs. It is the memory of Carlotta that creates Madeleine, and the memory of Madeleine that recreates Judy. In the end, we tend to wonder about the body that has been finally dismissed: is it Judy's or Madeleine's or Carlotta's?

Madeleine is a perfect archetype of an ideal woman: soft-spoken, refined, elusive, and urbane. She has a dream-like aura about her: forbidding, and yet alluring. Scottie wants his woman to be just like Madeleine. He, therefore, sets about recreating a real woman after his image of a perfect woman. Judy's dark hair, her bright dresses, her deportment, and her countenance are gradually transformed. The refashioning and re-dressing of Judy bring forth "the socially constructed nature of all forms of dress" (Spooner 2004, 4). The real Judy is lost behind the clothes, the color of the hair, and the makeup plastered on her. Catherine Spooner's observation that "[t]he so-called 'natural' body is always filtered through the dual lens of fashion and artistic convention" (2004, 3) is an apt way of describing the gradually transforming body of Judy Barton. In *Vertigo*, the dresses selected by Scottie Ferguson take on almost the function of the skin of Judy. The muted demeanor of Madeleine becomes prominent as Judy's vibrancy gets subdued. This is made possible by the transference of Scottie's idea of Madeleine's fashion on Judy. Judy's "natural" frame is not only sieved and shaped through the fashion imposed by Scottie. Judy's frame disappears completely and what remains on screen is the artistry intended by her creator. The cosmetic surface becomes the self and the previous body is slowly erased. Unlike the first half of the film, where Judy (under the tutelage of Gavin Elster) had replaced an imaginary Madeleine; in the second half, Judy (on Scottie's insistence) is ironically "replenished" by the illusory Madeleine.

Memory and a created nostalgia are used as patriarchal tools to create a tame ideal female anatomy.

With the annihilation of the memory comes the annihilation of the body. That Judy's body is dispensable, that it only serves as a repository of memories of another body becomes clear as she falls into the abyss and her body disappears from the screen and Scottie stands on the edge looking down at the ruined remnants of his self-created image. Memory and what it entails takes a grotesque form in the final shot of *Vertigo* as we stand with Scottie at the precipice; we do not see but only imagine the mangled body of Judy, a product of the warped psyches of the two men in her life.

Obsession with the memory of a body and its preservation explored in *Vertigo* is taken a step further in Hitchcock's next shocker *Psycho*, where Norma Bates and Marion Crane become victims of yet another obsessive character trapped in his world of self-created memories. Unlike Judy's live body, it is Norma Bates' wasted corpse that becomes a repository of Norman's idyllic past in *Psycho*. Norma Bates and Madeleine Elster become symbolic representations of our conflicting reactions to a taxidermist's creation. We are petrified of Norma and we are fascinated by Madeleine—two persons who exist only in our minds—two persons who are not there: just like Norman Bates' stuffed birds that are there and yet not there, the ones whom we watch with mesmerizing dread and fascination.

The idea of an absent/imagined body and a constant, futile effort at preserving it is a recurrent feature of Hitchcock's films. Scottie's attempts at re-creating Madeleine in Judy, Norman's attempts at taming a vibrant Marion and a terrifying mother, and Hitchcock's unending attempts of creating a beautiful and obedient anatomy in his female actors may all be seen as a continuous narrative of a series of male creators trying desperately to resurrect a female body that exists in their mind. Judy Barton in *Vertigo*, Marion, Norman, and Norma Bates in *Psycho*, and the real-life Tippi Hedren—all carry the literal and/or figurative connotations of taxidermized remade bodies. The bodies employed in these films have the common property of acting almost like tombs that carry the memories of other bodies. Taxidermy is a perfect art that fits the requirement of a director who wants to stage dramas of created memories and desires that desperately seek permanence in a "perfect" female anatomy.

"I Think Only Birds Look Well Stuffed because ... They're Kind of Passive, to Begin with"—Norman

Rachel Poliquin in *The Breathless Zoo* (2012), while discussing the futility of capturing beauty that is not alive, speaks of the exotic hummingbirds (an American import) collected and preserved in Liverpool Museum by William Bullock in the late 1790s (43–4). The blending of death and beauty makes such exhibits sites of eternal longing. The idea of preserving the materiality of a beautiful object in permanent repose necessitates its destruction at the height of its comeliness. Perhaps that is the tragedy of corporeality. Material beauty is so ephemeral that to capture it for posterity one needs to destroy it when it is at its peak of physical resplendence. But the preservation of such "dead beauty" also brings forth the futility of such preservation as death eliminates the very source of such beauty. The stuffed hummingbirds that were a raging fascination for the Victorians were ultimately sad artifacts of a failed attempt to capture the fleeting nature of animate beauty.

This delectable concoction of beauty and death, with a generous sprinkling of physical torture, has usually been a recipe of sure success for many of the Body Horrors. The very art of taxidermy could well have informed the genre of the corporeal Gothic in the sense that the impossibility of capturing and permanently possessing the "liveness" of beauty is what contributes significantly to the melancholic yet sensational high that a Body Gothic is famous for. The pathos lies in the fact that to witness a yearned-for beauty for a longer period, we destroy it and ironically remain satisfied with its replica. The very act of destruction defeats our desire as we replace a "life" with a "life-like." Poliquin, describing Victorian England's frenzy for the hummingbirds, thus rues: "The impossibility of witnessing life in a creature that was so profoundly lively intensified Victorians' infatuation with the little birds to a near-ecstatic romantic high" (2012, 48), which ironically "led to their destruction" (2012, 48). Here preservation, fascination, and destruction go hand in hand.

Hitchcock had significantly replaced animal stuffing in Bloch's novel with bird stuffing in his film *Psycho*. Norman is a taxidermist who recreates birds. Such substitution may acquire a sinister reading when we take into consideration the age-old popular analogy between "birds" and "women."³ Conventionally, patriarchy has always projected women as objects either to be ingested or to be incorporated. The parallels between "damsels in distress" and "vulnerable birds to be preyed upon" happen to be one of the staples of mainstream narrative cinema. In "The Representation of Violence to Women: Hitchcock's 'Frenzy'" (1985), the author Jeanne Thomas Allen, while discussing the rape-murder scene in *Frenzy* explains how the postures of Marion Crane in *Psycho* and Brenda in *Frenzy* were choreographed in a way that evokes the image of a bird at the moment of its yielding, with "their heads thrown backwards … back arched, neck extended" (33–4). Even before Marion is attacked, there are several occasions in the parlor scene where Marion looks alert as Norman questions her on her whereabouts. Her keen eyes, the tilt of her head, and her alert posture go quite well with Norman's observation, "You eat like a bird" (see Figure 3.1).

Psycho is replete with avian imagery: Norman's stuffed specimens in his parlor and his office, the sketches of birds in Marion's room in the motel, the victim in the shower who is significantly called Marion *Crane*—one who comes from *Phoenix*—a place named after a bird born out of its own ashes (reminding

Figure 3.1 Marion in the parlor scene, *Psycho*.

---

³ "Bird" is a casual British slang term used as a synonym for a young woman (usually an attractive promiscuous one), and Hitchcock must have been well aware of the term used thus.

us again of the idea of destruction and re-creation), and reference to Marion eating like a "bird." Even Norma Bates is preserved in a way that birds are preserved. Her skin has to undergo the conventional processes of being cut, dissected, and treated with preservatory materials like borax, salt, alcohol, and tanning oil. The head is kept intact as in the case of bird preservations, without the eyes, the brain, and the tongue. It is as if Hitchcock, through such effusion of bird imagery, prepares us for his next feature, *The Birds* (1963), a film where all his "stuffed birds" come alive to peck at his meticulous "creation": Tippi Hedren.

"For Each Man Kills the Thing He Loves": *The Birds*

It is generally believed that it was Hitchcock who culled a movie star out of a "small-time model" Tippi Hedren. From her wardrobe to her hairstyle, from her eating habits to the company she should keep, from her body language to every nuance of her facial expressions—everything was minutely choreographed and designed and dictated by Hitchcock: "I controlled every movement on her face. She did purely cinematic acting of very fine shadings all the time. She wasn't allowed to do anything beyond what I gave her. It was my control entirely" (Hitchcock on Tippi Hedren, Spoto 1999, 470). Tippi conceded to what Hitchcock had claimed: "Melanie Daniels is his character … He gives his actors very little leeway. He'll listen, but he has a very definite plan in mind as to how he wants his characters to act" (Moral 2013b, 64–5).

However, it was not only Tippi's performance that Hitchcock molded by his regular scripting and voice training. He was meticulously plotting and shaping her body as well. Tippi Hedren in *The Birds* had to become Melanie Daniels—an exquisitely dressed privileged socialite in her mid-twenties. But Hitchcock desired to create "Melanie Daniels" in the molds of someone else—Grace Kelly. Virginia Darcy, the hairstylist of Tippi in the film, informs: "He [Hitchcock] said he wanted her [Tippi] to look like Grace Kelly" (Moral 2013b, 78). Thus, Edith Head (dress designer), Helen Hunt, and Virginia Darcy (hairdressers) set out to carve a "Grace Kelly" out of a "Tippi Hedren"—her hair was dyed, her clothes were designed keeping Grace in mind, and since Tippi had different facial features from Grace, "Virginia had to create a new look that framed her face" (Moral 2013b, 79).

The cocktail dresses, the ball gowns (for pre-shooting trials), the famous light green suit,[4] the mink coat, the jewelry (a mesh bracelet watch, a ring, and a neckpiece of baby pearls), and "the upswept trademark hairstyle" (Moral 2013b, 78) of Melanie Daniels are all examples of a metaphoric taxidermized Re-Creation. Tippi Hedren, under the garb of Melanie Daniels, was being remade into the filmmaker's desired anatomy of Grace Kelly (reminding us of Scottie Ferguson's attempts of transforming Judy Barton into Madeleine Elster in *Vertigo*). Tony Lee Moral quotes Virginia Darcy: "Hitchcock wanted Tippi to look very sophisticated like a high-class lady. As he wanted her to look like Grace Kelly, we had to color her hair a lighter shade of blonde. We gave it special coloring, not peroxide, but Clairol, which is used in the salons today" (Moral 2013b, 78–9). This, again, is uncannily similar to Scottie transforming Judy from a brunette to a blonde in *Vertigo*.

The subtle, but gradually more pronounced, marks of Hitchcock's proprietorship became evident as he tried to control Tippi Hedren off the screen as well. She was kept under constant vigilance much to the bewilderment of Hedren: "He started telling me what I should wear on my own time, what I should be eating, and what friends I should be seeing" (Spoto 1999, 456). As Edith Head confirms, dresses were designed both for on-screen and off-screen appearances of Tippi Hedren (Moral 2013b, 80). A thoroughly confused Hedren muses: "I had always heard that his idea was to take a woman—usually a blond—and break her apart ... but I thought this was only in the plots of his films" (Spoto 1999, 457). She cannot be at fault if she had already apprehended that such was not the case with her.

The Birds, adapted from a short story by Daphne du Maurier, depicts a world out of control that almost borders on an apocalypse, where thousands of birds attack a sleepy little village near Bodega Bay. The attacks coincide

---

[4] Apart from the pet shop scene, Tippi Hedren throughout *The Birds* wears this green dress made by Cristobal Balenciaga and Charles Creed. Rita Riggs recollects, "Hitchcock loved green and specifically chose the shade celadon. Celadon is a term for ceramics, invented in ancient China, and is a light shade of green. Grace Kelly had worn a celadon-green, mid-length jacket with collar and matching skirt in *Rear Window* (1954)" (Moral 2013b, 91). We may recall, both Madeleine and Judy wear green when Scottie first sees them in *Vertigo*.

with the arrival of a wealthy socialite, Melanie Daniels (Tippi Hedren) at Bodega Bay where she has come with the precise intention of meeting and befriending an attractive young lawyer Mitch Brenner (Rod Taylor). The film then revolves around the twin turmoil that happens both within and without the Brenner family with Melanie trying to disrupt the order and hierarchy of the Brenner family, and hordes of birds trying to invade and shatter a town. *The Birds* was also a cause of personal anxiety for Hitchcock, especially after *Psycho*. The terror of *The Birds* had to outdo even that of *Psycho*: "Our intention, he [Hitchcock] told me, was simply to scare the hell out of people. Even more than he had done in *Psycho*, he said he wanted to arouse intense emotions from his audience" (Evan Hunter on the making of *The Birds*, Spoto 1999, 449). Moreover, the central character Melanie Daniels (Tippi Hedren) had already become an object of obsession for Hitchcock.[5] The time was thus right for the kill. Thus, emerged *The Birds*, with its near-fatal attack on Tippi Hedren. The script, initially drafted, had Annie (Suzanne Pleshette) as the victim of the birds. Hitchcock later decided to make Melanie (Tippi) the object of the attic attack, instead of Annie (Moral 2013b, 138).

The attack is staged thus: Melanie Daniels, trapped in the Brenner house, trying to protect the family from the rage of violent birds, climbs up to the attic and is brutally attacked and injured by hundreds of birds. Donald Spoto describes the entire ordeal in *The Dark Side of Genius* (1999):

> Two men, wearing protective gloves and carrying huge cartons, were carefully positioned—one on each side of the camera, facing the actress, who stood against a wall. The entire set was enclosed in a giant cage and then, as Hedren waved her arms and fought them off, live birds were thrown at her while the cameras rolled. "There was no precedent for anything like this, and no one knew what to expect," she recalled. "All of us thought that it could be done very quickly—and no one hoped so more than I." But the shooting continued throughout the day. Birds were hurled at her; frightened, they flew away as she defended herself against the gulls and crows with wild, increasingly honest and unacted gestures of terror.
>
> (458)

---

[5] See Spoto's *The Dark Side of Genius* (1999, 449–79) for details.

This trial continued for five days. Spoto recalls Jessica Tandy's (Lydia Brenner in *The Birds*) words: "for an entire week, the poor woman put up with that. She was alone in that caged room, acting, with the birds coming at her" (Spoto 1999, 459). On the fourth day of the shooting, Hedren recounts:

> And so on Thursday the wardrobe mistress took me into my dressing room, where elastic bands were tied around my body, with nylon thread that was pulled through tiny holes in my costume. I soon found out what this was for. One leg of each bird was tied to each piece of string, so that when I lay on the floor they couldn't fly away but would bound and perch all over me. This went on for the rest of the day.
>
> (Spoto 1999, 459–60)

The final attack of the birds in the film is a re-enactment of the shower scene of *Psycho*. Only this time the knife has been replaced by crows and seagulls. Birds—real ones—would peck at her, scratch her, and gash the lower lid of her left eye: "the direction was that she must keep her eyes open as if in a trance ... one of the birds jumped from Tippi's shoulder over her face and nearly clawed her eye," Rita Riggs reports, "I think the last time she managed to stay still, keep her eyes open, I remember a crow walked right across and near her eye, thank God she didn't move and we got the shot" (Moral 2013b, 142–3). Ray Berwick, the bird trainer adds, "'It's a miracle she got through it with her face intact" (Moral 2013b, 141)—a face that Hitchcock along with his hairdressers and costume designers had carefully crafted. Tippi suffered a complete breakdown after this ordeal. According to Spoto, during this time, Hitchcock was often heard saying to interviewers: "To paraphrase Oscar Wilde, 'You destroy the thing you love'" (1999, 460).

Tony Lee Moral disagrees with this popular verdict: "Contrary to popular opinion in the press, he [Hitchcock] didn't unleash the fury of the birds on Tippi out of sadism or spite. He was getting the job done and, in doing so, secured Tippi cinematic immortality just like he did for Janet Leigh in the shower scene in *Psycho*" (2013b, 141). The attic attack of *The Birds* was one of the cinematic highs of Hitchcock, like the shower attack of *Psycho*. Again, like the shower attack, this scene was heavily dependent on montage—the snipping and splicing of small pieces of film to get the desired effect. To achieve fifty seconds of screen time, Hitchcock had to shoot for a week. Hitchcock informs: "What you will see on the screen will be a mosaic of little pieces of film—some of them less than an inch long" (Moral 2013b, 140). Both the shower scene and the attic scene are thus assemblages as snippets of films are rearranged and patched together to create Hitchcock's notorious, violent set pieces.

While constructing these highly disturbing scenes, Moral does admit that Hitchcock tends to forget that his actors are real people and at times treats them like "puppets" (2013, 141). In keeping with this simile of a puppet, Hitchcock used a body double of Tippi Hedren in the aftermath of the attic attack as Mitch brings Melanie down the attic because Tippi was too ill to perform the scene (reminding us of Marion's body double in the shower scene). The required close shots of Tippi's face were later inserted in those scenes (Moral 2013b, 143). Another instance of a body replaced, disassembled, and reassembled on screen.

While *Psycho* deals with dead birds, *The Birds* deals with live ones. The prey in *Psycho* becomes the predator in *The Birds*. A total of 25,000 birds were used in the film that included crows, seagulls, sparrows, finches, and ducks (Moral 2013b, 104). The bodies of these birds were also restructured and "managed" to accommodate the demands of the film. Black silk hoods covered the crows' heads to render them temporarily blind to prevent them from flying away in the School Attack scene. Tiny magnets were attached to their feet to make them roost on the school terrace. Pins were attached to the seagulls' beaks that made them pierce the balloons at the Brenner house party. A sparrow's wings were tied with a little elastic band to prevent it from flying away at the beginning of the Sparrow Attack scene. Rubber tips were attached to the beaks of some crows and seagulls in the Attic Attack scene. As mentioned earlier, small elastic bands were attached to the feet of some birds in the same scene. Cardboard cut-outs, taxidermized birds, hammers with fake bird heads, and a dummy seagull were also used at several crucial stages of the film.[6] Hitchcock and his bird trainers refashioned the birds' anatomies in a manner that brings

---

[6] See *The Making of Hitchcock's Birds* (Morals 2013b, 92–140) for a detailed discussion on the birds and the choreography of their attacks in *The Birds*.

to mind the refashioning of Tippi's anatomy in the film. The dead birds and the dead Mother of the Bates world in *Psycho* are replaced by live re-formed birds and a live re-formed female protagonist at Bodega Bay in *The Birds*.

The Victorian house, famous for its insularity, in *Psycho,* may find faint echoes in the isolated Brenner House of Bodega Bay. The initial openness of the bay, the sea, the wind, and the bright sky gradually narrow down to the confines of the Brenner House. The Brenner House is transformed into a cage twice in the film. In the Sparrow Attack scene, 1,500 sparrows and finches, confined in opaque cages, were made to escape through trap doors and through the chimney into the living room of the Brenners which had already been wrapped by plastic sheets to prevent the birds from escaping (Moral 2013b, 128–9). Again, the attic was literally converted into a cage where the birds were made to attack Tippi. All these actors (human and avian) were trapped and frightened. In this film, Hitchcock brilliantly captures the irony inherent in fear where both the prey and the predator are petrified of each other. While the predators "seemed more terrified themselves than threatening" (Moral 2013b, 130), the victim reciprocated with "increasingly honest and unacted gestures of terror" (Spoto 1999, 458). The bathroom, the basement, and the attic (the hidden or neglected spaces usually situated at the fringes of a house) become Hitchcock's cages/stages where he preserves through his films the menace of random violence. These are Hitchcock's dioramas, his workshops as well as his "dolls' houses."

"I Cannot Bear to Be Handled": *Marnie*

Marnie was a film that was to follow *Psycho* instead of *The Birds*—a film that was supposed to be a comeback venture of Grace Kelly (after her marriage to the Prince of Monaco). Much to Hitchcock's disappointment, Kelly refused and the film was shelved. Hitchcock again returned to *Marnie* after *The Birds* and Tippi Hedren was his obvious choice for the lead role. Spoto describes *Marnie* as Hitchcock's most "personal motion picture," one that discloses his "personal touches," his "obsessions," and "the array of memories, fantasies, and images" (468). Based on Winston Graham's novel of the same name, *Marnie* is the story of a beautiful, elusive, and frigid kleptomaniac (Tippi Hedren) starved of her mother's (Bernice Edgar, played by Louise Latham) love, and alternately "loved" and violated by her husband Mark Rutland (Sean Connery).

Marnie is replete with animal imagery and references. Marnie's love for and self-identification with her horse Forio, her staying at the Red Fox Tavern, her gifting a "real mink" wrap to her mother, the children singing "the lady with the alligator purse" on the street, Mark's reading the book *Animals of the Seashore* just before he rapes Marnie, his interest in a Kenyan flower which is called phattid bugs, Mark's banter that Marnie has the scent of a horse that will impress his father, his taming of a jaguarundi cat named Sophie, and the prolonged fox-hunt sequence, all point to the hunter-hunted motif of the film. Most of the Marnie-Mark exchanges center around animals. The first time that they are alone together, Mark acquaints Marnie with the photograph of a jaguarundi cat, Sophie, whom Mark claims to have tamed:

> Mark: That's Sophie. She's a jaguarundi. I trained her.
> Marnie: Oh, what did you train her to do?
> Mark: To trust me.
> Marnie: Is that all?
> Mark: That's a great deal for a jaguarundi.

This is followed by Mark's asking Marnie to type a piece from his manuscript on the "predators of the Brazilian rain forest." He informs Marnie that his original vocation was of a zoologist. But it is Marnie who for the first time explicitly connects human and nonhuman species here:

> Marnie: Does zoology include people, Mr. Rutland?
> Mark: Well, in a way, it includes all the animal ancestors from whom man derived his instincts.
> Marnie: Lady's instincts too?
> Mark: That paper deals with the instincts of predators, what you might call the criminal class of the animal world – lady animals figure very largely as predators.

The early part of the film quite explicitly compares Marnie to a predator—a beautiful thief who steals from unsuspecting lecherous employers. The film opens with a close shot of a yellow leather purse and as the camera remains static, a woman carrying the purse walks away from the camera on a railway platform. We do not see her face. We only get a full view of her back and her dark hair. The next scene takes us to a robbed office where a distraught Mr. Strutt (Martin Gable) gives his statement to the police. He describes the thief in the following manner: "Five feet five, hundred and ten pounds, size eight dress, blue eyes, black wavy hair, even features, good teeth." Even before we see her, Marnie comes to us as a body with a detailed catalog of her size, weight, and facial features. Mark Rutland enters immediately after this description and adds, "the brunette with the legs." And a few scenes later Lil (Diane Baker), Mark's sister-in-law, calls her "a dish." The age-old analogy repeats itself—an attractive woman to be ingested or consumed, one whose weight, size, and legs have been carefully measured. The predator, as we see, is relegated to the position of a prey. David Greven in *Intimate Violence* (2014) connects Marnie to the wretched fox who is preyed upon and torn to pieces by a huge group of hounds in the fox-hunt sequence of the film: "the fox hunt is depicted as absurdly grandiose, with phalanxes of predators pursuing so small a prey … Marnie's resilience emerges from her empathetic connection to the violated animal. Like the fox, Marnie is pursued and hunted by the demands of the social order" (202–3).

Marnie is compared to our nonhuman co-habitants of the earth in another subtle way. The two species that intrigue Mark the most are jaguarundis and phattid bugs. A significant feature shared by both these species is their ability to camouflage. "A mysterious hunter from a surprising lineage," jaguarundis have a "grey and reddish coloration [that] keeps them hidden from predators and prey" (Dubeau and Strapp 2022, 7:48). Again, phattid bugs are explained to Marnie by Mark in the following way:

> In Africa in Kenya, there is quite a beautiful flower. It is coral-colored with little tipped green blossoms, rather like a hyacinth. If you reach out to touch it you would discover that the flower is not a flower at all, but a design made up of hundreds of tiny insects called phattid bugs. They escape the eyes of hungry birds by living and dying in the shape of a flower.

Marnie has several social security cards with names as varied as Marion Holland, Mary Taylor, Margaret Edgar, and Peggy Nicolson. She appears first on screen as a brunette. In the hotel room, she washes the color off and becomes a blonde. Later we find her mother commenting on her hair being dyed light blonde (a shade she does not approve of). So, even the viewers are not quite sure what is the real color of Marnie's hair. Only Marnie and her mother know the real color of her hair. She changes her hair, her style of clothes, accessories, and names and slides from one identity into another as she robs her employers of their cash. Like jaguarundis and phattid bugs, she excels in the art of disguise until a zoologist (Mark) discovers her true identity. The zoologist is, however, keen on keeping his discovered "specimen" to himself. The following exchange gives us a clear idea of the nature of their relationship:

> Marnie: You don't love me! I am just something you've caught. You think I'm some kind of animal you've trapped.
> Mark: That's right, you are. I've caught something really wild this time, haven't I? I've tracked you and caught you and by God, I'm gonna keep you.

Like Sophie, the jaguarundi, Marnie becomes Mark's new "difficult-to-train" feline pet. As he lightly states, in a completely different context, "I'll just go on calling you Marnie … that's easily explained pet name."

Hitchcock decides that this "pet" should be raped by her "owner." Spoto relates Hitchcock's plan for *Marnie* based on the director's taped conversation with scriptwriter Evan Hunter where Hitchcock insists that Marnie be raped by her husband on the second night of their honeymoon cruise. Despite Hunter's objections that such an unmotivated and unnecessary addition would mar the image of the husband, Hitchcock maintained that the rape scene had to be inserted in the script and he insisted "that at the exact moment of the rape he wanted the camera right on her shocked face" (469).[7] We can well understand the familiar pattern here—"the story of a director's desire for an inaccessible actress who, therefore, became, even more, an object of fantasy" (Spoto 1999, 472).

The constricted close shots of Hedren's face and the close-up of pressing lips on the second night of their honeymoon where Mark forces himself on Marnie

---

7 Hunter was dismissed by Hitchcock from the film because of this difference of opinion.

impart to *Marnie* the feel of an exploitation film. *Psycho* was a rehearsal of what Hitchcock had in store for us. Marnie's first assumed name is Marion. Like Marion in *Psycho*, she has stolen cash from her boss and is on the run. The death of Marion and the physical abuse of Marnie share an important likeness. The phallic knife and the screaming orifice of Marion in *Psycho*, labeled as symbolic rape by scholars like George Toles[8] transmutes into a real rape in *Marnie* where not only Marnie's husband Mark, but the camera, and the man who directs the camera become willing agents of violence. The only way to tame, contain, and preserve an "elusive wild thing" permanently is to "desecrate" it first.

The entire film may be seen as Marnie's struggle not to give up her untamed nature to a person who could go to any lengths (even rape) to acquire and keep her. Although Robin Wood has expressed his doubt whether Mark indeed knew that he was raping Marnie (Greven 2014, 206), a reading that comes as a surprise since Marnie has never given enthusiastic consent to Mark's advances throughout the film. David Greven states:

> In many ways, Mark abducts Marnie, cutting her off from all she knows ... His actions proceed from the basis of his physical and emotional desires to possess Marnie sexually ... intellectually and ... emotionally as well ... It is precisely because he continues to force her to submit to him sexually despite his intimate knowledge of her revulsion toward the sex act and his genuine feelings of tenderness for her, feelings he expresses physically in the moment when he places his own robe around her naked body, that the scene is so devastating—and absolutely crucial to the film and to Hitchcock's body of work.
>
> (2014, 210)

Tony Lee Moral and David Greven speak of Mark's vulnerability in this scene. Mark, like Norman, is a susceptible insecure man. As a successful white male entrepreneur in twentieth-century urban America, he plays along the acquisitive rules of proprietorship. Greven attempts a queer reading of *Marnie* where Mark desperately tries to function as a guardian of a heteronormative patriarchal structure.

---

[8] See "'If Thine Eye Offend Thee' ... *Psycho* and the Art of Infection" by George Toles (2013, 159–74).

It cannot be denied that Marnie was raped. Although Hitchcock and Jay Presson Allan do not call the act "rape" (Moral 2013a, 209), we the viewers, can well discern the look of trance-like endurance on Marnie's face. Marnie endures the sexual act because she has no other choice. And that is rape. The moment when Mark, in an attempt to soothe her, kisses her, we are ironically and quite disconcertingly reminded of another attack—the attack on Melanie Daniels by the birds in the attic in Hitchcock's previous film—*The Birds*.

Figure 3.2 Mark kissing Marnie in the rape scene, *Marnie*.

Figure 3.3 A bird attacking Melanie in the attic scene, *The Birds*.

Sheer terror can manifest itself in many ways—through scream or silence, through frantic struggle, or petrified stillness. Mark, knowingly (as Spoto and Greven suggest) or unknowingly (as Wood and Allan suggest) becomes a predator—the "hungry bird" who could detect the "phattid bug."

David Greven puts forward an excellent analysis of Mark's act of "generosity" in this controversial scene:

> the tenderness Mark demonstrates toward Marnie is not only inextricable from but demonstrative of his desire to possess her. Indeed, it indicates he believes that he does possess her … Mark does not pick up Marnie's robe and put it back on her; he puts *his* robe on Marnie's body. To have put her robe back on her would have been to acknowledge his wrongdoing and attempt to atone for this invasive action. Placing his robe on her signifies his belief that she is his possession.
>
> (Greven 2014, 212)

Unclothing a body and then reclothing it has strong connections with the art of taxidermy. Taking off the outer covering of a body and then refashioning the body in a manner that the creator deems fit is how the art functions. By draping Marnie with his clothes, Mark is imposing a part of himself on her. It is in keeping with the practice of branding or inking a newly acquired body. Such branding suggests power over the body coupled with the fear of losing the body. Mark's attempts at possession do not end here as he penetrates further into Marnie's childhood memories. He does not rest until she confronts her troubled past at the end of the film. He ransacks her body and mind to bring her within the comforting folds of an assuring patriarchy. It is, as Mark himself states, his "moral responsibility." A successful American man who revived his father's failing business has to own what he likes and remold it further to like it even better.

For Alfred Hitchcock, remolding usually comes through the medium of his moving camera. It is his motion picture that would preserve the creation of tamed anatomies and the on-screen violence meted out to them. He could freeze motion in "motion" reminding us ironically that "cinema's living and moving bodies are simply animated stills" (*Death 24x a Second: Stillness and the Moving Image*, Laura Mulvey 2006, 90).

4

Hitchcock's Installation: *Psycho*'s Shower Stabbing, *Frenzy*'s Serial Strangling, and the Beginning of Slashers

"Here the fairies play!"—*Psycho* and Hitchcock's Diorama

In an effort to eternize a face he found fascinating; Alfred Hitchcock had once attempted to freeze that face in time. Using a complex make-up session as an excuse, he created a life-like mask of Tippi Hedren and preserved it for days. He also sent an intriguing and disturbing gift to Hedren's five-year-old daughter—"an elaborate and expensive doll of her mother dressed as the character she played in *The Birds*, complete with a miniature green suit and elegant coiffure"—enclosed in a tiny pine-box (Spoto 1999, 467). This effort at arresting the ephemeral finds a concrete filmic form in Alfred Hitchcock's *Psycho*. *Psycho* is replete with the ideas of a body being replicated, destroyed, recreated, and redestroyed. The film explores every aspect of what we can do to a vulnerable body and to what extent we can go with it. From using a body double for Janet Leigh in the shower scene to the stuffed bodies of birds generously littered in the motel office, to the empty eye sockets of a long-dead mother, Hitchcock seems to create his kind of taxidermy with the body of the film.

The film is breathtakingly fast-paced, with the plot thickening from the very beginning, and abruptly seeming to come to a standstill with the murder of the protagonist. Just when we completely identify with Marion, she is ruthlessly killed, much to the bewilderment of the viewer. The knife not only rips Marion apart, but it also slashes the corpus of the film's narrative and is restored through the shell of another character, Norman Bates, with whom we momentarily identify and then realize, much to our horror, that the shell of

Norman contains the vengeful mother within. The ultimate disillusionment comes when the empty eye sockets of Norma Bates stare at us. Her immobility and her helplessness come home to us as we realize that we too are immobile and helpless as we watch, with a mixture of curiosity and squeamishness, the craft of a director who creates, destroys, recreates and redestroys the viewers' reactions by alternately filling, emptying, refilling, and then re-emptying the bodies of the major characters as well as the body of the film.[1]

Psycho was planned on a shoestring budget where Hitchcock used his television crew for shooting and the film was completed in forty-two days. Only two men, Saul Bass and Bernard Herrmann, came expensive. The slashing bars of the credit sequence and the slashing chords of Herrmann's music in *Psycho* had the effect of flaying the corpus of the film at the very outset. Raymond Durgnat's detailed description of the credit sequence in *A Long Hard Look at Psycho* (2002) gives us a feeling that someone is splitting, slashing, skinning, and grappling his way into the narrative:

> The Paramount logo fades to a black screen, which turns light grey as music starts: chunky staccato chords under keening violins. From the right-hand edge, black stripes stretch across the screen; more appear, at unpredictable heights, till they block the screen like a window–blind. Against the last bands, streaking across at middle height, white angular flecks appear … and turn out to be the *tips* and *tails* of letters, *slashed* laterally and vertically disaligned. The "window blind" *breaks* up as more black bands *thrust* in, *pushing* the last grey strips off left. The bits of letters click together, to read … "Alfred Hitchcock's." Uncompleted syntax holds the screen for a full two seconds, until the letters' middle stratum skids left, *pursued* by more grey bands, which *amass* in a tight, though still staggered, formation … New shards of letters slide in … On the now black background, the *scattering* of broken letters slide and *snap* together, spelling "Psycho," for about two seconds, until that word, too, *cracks* into three strata.
>
> (Durgnat 2002, 19, emphasis added)

---

[1] Philip J. Skerry gives us a bewildering, and almost amusing, list of identities of the killer in *Psycho*: "What is different about *Psycho* is that in other films, it is almost always a guy killing a woman, but in *Psycho* it is a woman killing a woman; but then, of course, it isn't a woman killing a woman; it is a man dressed up as a woman killing a woman. But it is really a woman killing a woman, because Tony Perkins was in New York when the scene was being filmed, so they had a stand-in for him—a woman. Makes your head swim!" (2008, 187).

The verbs used generously by Durgnat, like "stretch," "slashed," "breaks," "thrust," "push," "pursued," "scattering," "snap," "and cracks" eerily bring forth the images of breaking, making, re-breaking, and remaking of a body. The black and grey stripes of the credit sequence act as knives that split and scatter the letters. The letters that form the words "Alfred Hitchcock's" and "Psycho" themselves may be treated as bodies—they first appear as "white angular flecks" that later develop "tips" and "tails"—bodies that are "slashed laterally and vertically disaligned" until the "bits of letters" (like bits of skin and bits of bones) are "clicked together" to form the name of the creator. The "middle stratum" of the letters "Alfred Hitchcock's" then "skids" only to form "a—mass" that is "tight" and yet "staggered." This is followed by "new shards of letters" that "slide" in—reminding us of "a mass," a mass of flesh that can only "slide" in. Finally, the "scattering of broken letters" (like broken joints and bones and bits of flesh) "slide and snap together" to form the name of the creation, until that too "cracks into three strata." The creation, destruction, recreation, and re-destruction begin from the very beginning: from the film to the filmmaker to the viewer—no one is spared.

We may now move on from Saul Bass to Bernard Herrmann, from the slashing bars to the slashing chords of *Psycho*. From the credit sequence Bernard Hermann starts creating his kind of slashing: "chunky staccato bursts with keening violin" is how Durgnat describes it (Durgnat 2002, 19). Joseph Stefano's reactions, as stated by Jack Sullivan, when he heard Herrmann's score for *Psycho* is interesting: "When I first heard it, I realized what he'd done. He'd taken everybody's guts and used them for music" (Sullivan 2006, 243). His "anxious violas" when Marion dresses to flee from her Phoenix apartment, the "whispered tremolos and harmonics" just before Arbogast is stabbed, the "languid chords" sweeping across the Phoenix sky as the camera pans and enters the private space of lovers, the "desolate chords" while Norman cleans Marion's blood followed by the "madhouse cue,"[2] the cue that first peeps its head when Marion suggests to Norman that his mother should be institutionalized, rears its head in the mop-up scene, slithers menacingly around the female voice-

---

[2] The phrases "languid chords," "desolate chords," "Madhouse cue" (2006, 257), "anxious violas," "whispered tremolos and harmonics" (2006, 250) are used by Jack Sullivan in *Hitchcock's Music* to describe the desolation that *Psycho's* music inspires.

over of Norman as he states "she wouldn't even harm a fly," and finally dies out slowly in the final dissolve of the swamp: dense, stark, jagged, and brutal, yet somehow creating an atmosphere of abject loneliness in which every character is trapped.

While the strings of Herrmann tighten and become fiercer in the shower scene with the repeated slashing down of the knife (coupled with the repeated onslaught of swift violent cuts on screen), the viewers along with Marion, unable to grasp the absurdity and randomness of such violence, hopelessly try to "claw" their way out. Jack Sullivan in *Hitchcock's Music* (2006) depicts Bernard Hermann's music as a surrogate of the knife itself:

> In addition to being viscerally terrifying on their own, the slashing glissandos seem to stand in for the stabbing knife and Marion's cries—as well as our own … Sight and sound are insidiously united; Hitchcock's devastating montage seems cut with a musical knife, Herrmann's stabbings launching the attack.
>
> (255)

Music in both the murder scenes (of Marion and Arbogast) is closely associated with the movement of the knife. Hitchcock also speaks of this close collaboration between the swift cuts of the camera, the attack of the murderer, and the music that jars the senses during the killing of Arbogast:

> the main reason for raising the camera so high was to get the contrast between the long shot and the close-up of the big head as the knife came down at him. It was like music, you see, the high shot with the violins, and suddenly the big head with the brass instruments clashing. In the high shot, the mother dashes out and I cut into the movement of the knife sweeping down.
>
> (*Hitchcock/ Truffaut* 1984, 276)

Herrmann's jagged slashing chords come back again when Lila discovers Norma Bates' preserved corpse in the basement. There is no escape from these sometimes melancholic, sometimes violent shrieks of Herrmann's strings. We are trapped in this mad world of string bows where the attack may come from any quarter: the swooping down of a random predator/creator over an unsuspecting creature that just happens to be at the wrong place at the wrong time.

From relentless movements between "the dense seventh and ninth chords" (Sullivan 2006, 254) *Psycho* leads us forcefully to stillness and silence. Music and silence have been meticulously planned to bring out both the terror of music and the dread of silence at their utmost pitch, suggesting respectively the rhythm of a pulsating live body and the silence and shuffling of a hollow carcass: "The most unforgettable silence follows the shower murder. Shuddering basses collapse with Marion, a deathlike silence splashed by the running shower, suggesting the tragedy of a young life down the drain" (Sullivan 2006, 251). After the unnerving desolate strings in the post-murder cleaning scene, the quietness that follows while Marion's car sinks slowly into the swamp is equally jarring. Finally, as against expectation, when Norma Bates' empty eye sockets reflect the light of the bulb in the basement, we encounter no brutal bursts of the string bow, but rather a dead silence, only pierced a moment later by Lila's shriek combined with Herrmann's shrill slashing chord as Norman Bates enters screaming, "I am Norma Bates!" The high-pitched piercing chord of Herrmann almost drowns the mad scream of Norman making us realize that we have finally witnessed the bewildering depths of the insane Bates world. The juxtaposition of sound and silence, rhythm and stillness make up the perfect recipe for Hitchcock's and Herrmann's shocker. After the initial fight for life, the struggles, and the shrieks, comes silence—the mark of surrender—the yielding of one's body to the predator.

"Their Death in My Hands"—Hitchcock's Installation

Psycho may be seen as Alfred Hitchcock's diorama where the fragmentation of the human body is followed by a passionate but violent reconstitution of it. Norma Bates, the preserved corpse of Norman Bates' mother, is perhaps one of the most ill-treated corpses we have encountered. She is not only ill-preserved; she is also ill-represented. She does not come across as a nurturing mother. She is cruel. She is mad. She is physically sick. She kills. And she is also dead. She is a woman who murders posthumously without even being granted the thrill of being a vampire, or a ghost. She is a "plain," "ugly," old, diseased, "unwomanly" woman who kills to "protect" her son from attractive young women. Her neighbors have long forgotten her. And much to her dismay her obsessed son has not. His act of remembering is so acute that he reconstructs her and kills in her name. Finally, a time comes when she grins through her son and places the blame rightfully on his shoulders, and Norman has to pay the price for messing with her body.

Messing with dead bodies is something Hitchcock loves doing. From his comic treatment of a dead body in *The Trouble with Harry* (1955) where the corpse refuses to remain hidden and crops up at inopportune moments to the gruesome littering of naked female corpses at every nook and corner of London in *Frenzy* (1972), from the ever-absent-but-potently-present dead body of Rebecca in *Rebecca* (1940) to the brooding existence of a corpse at a dinner gathering in *Rope* (1948), Hitchcock's fascination with dead bodies is a constant. *Psycho* also has a beautiful young corpse, sprawled naked over a dazzlingly white washroom. Unlike Norma Bates, who is carefully preserved by her son, Marion's body is wiped off the screen. The post-murder cleaning scene and Norman's painstaking efforts of removing every trace of her existence from the motel room are the absolute opposite of the treatment that Norma Bates' body receives. Marion's body is sucked into the swamp. But post-murder, Hitchcock does not simply make her disappear. The camera lingers to focus on the shower head, the curtain, the blood trickling down the drain and Marion's face pressed against the sterile white floor. The camera (apparently aimless) explores a place where no signs of life remain. The absolute silence after Bernard Herrmann's shrieking background score and the slow caressing camera movement after the onslaught of rapid cuts during the murder do nothing to soothe us. It remains one of the most disturbing post-crime scenes which the viewers are allowed to witness first.

Hitchcock in his book-length interview with Truffaut titled *Hitchcock/Truffaut* (1984), describes the shower scene in the following manner:

> It took us seven days to shoot that scene, and there were seventy camera setups for forty-five seconds of footage. We had a *torso* specially made

up for that scene ... but I didn't use it. I used a *live girl* instead, a *naked model* who stood in for Janet Leigh. We only showed Miss Leigh's *hands, shoulders*, and *head*. All the rest was the *stand-in*. Naturally, the knife never touched the body; it was all done in the montage. I shot some of it in slow motion so as to *cover* the breasts. The slow shots were not accelerated later on because they were inserted in the montage so as to give an impression of normal speed.

(1984, 277 emphases added)

As the bathroom door opens and a shadowy figure approaches the curtain, we only get flash views of the attacker and the knife and therefore cannot orient ourselves enough to create a defense. We are only shown the attacker for a split second and then we are turned away by the camera and must try to reorient ourselves again. How can Marion protect herself from a knife, or for that matter the murderer, whom she can never quite see? What the murderer does to Marion, the camera does to us. The camera is the agent of violence for the audience. However, Hitchcock's claims that the knife is not seen penetrating the skin for once stand contested as Philip J. Skerry in *Psycho in the Shower* (2008) rightly explicates, "there is a brief shot of the knife entering the flesh ... The shot is clearly evident in Richard Anobile's *Alfred Hitchcock's Psycho* in a blow-up of a frame from the shower scene that clearly shows the tip of the knife entering the flesh, with a clearly evident (and chilling) slit of the flesh" (224).

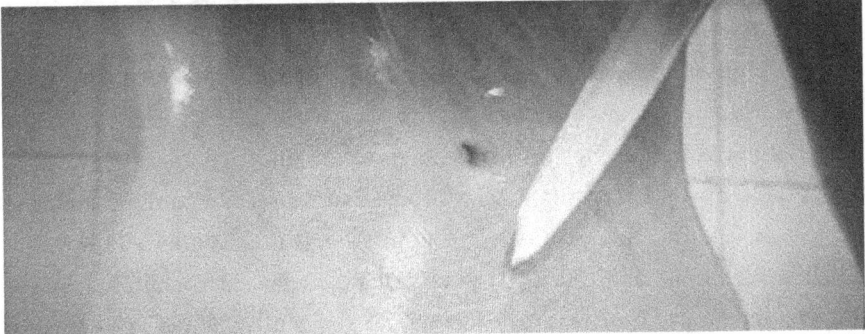

Figure 4.1 The knife touching Marion's torso, *Psycho*.

The spectacle of violence does not take place only on stage but is transferred to the stage of the viewer's mind and body; Hitchcock also makes the murder happen in our minds and our bodies.

Such imagined spectacles of pain problematize the relationship between the viewer and the viewed. While the dead and the mutilated become mere objects of prying and qualmishness, the viewer is not spared as well; he/she is placed both within and without that narrative of pain through the complex process of *seeing* as well as *feeling*. As Steven Bruhm in *Gothic Bodies: The Politics of Pain in Romantic Fiction* (1994), states: "[The] history of pain ... is in many ways a history of looking; it is a narrative of watching a pained object while occupying a contradictory space both *within* and *outside* that object" (xx). The viewer is placed in a porous zone where the subject, object, self, other, victim, predator, fiction, and reality seep into one another. Fred Botting, in search of a wider Gothic structure in *Limits of Horror* (2008), observes: "fiction and film cross into everyday life, displaying the permeable, shifting boundaries between reality and fantasy and enveloping every social position. We are all Frankensteins or monsters" (6). Botting's reading of the Gothic bodies suggests a merger between the created, the creator, and the viewer reminding us of Rachel Poliquin's reading of the taxidermy animal-object in *The Breathless Zoo* (2012) where the re-creation of an animal becomes a site of the creator's and the viewer's desire and yearning. The desecrated female bodies of *Psycho* and the re-created corpses of animals in taxidermy become agents, at times, of a violent heaving of those longings and angst back onto their creators as well as their viewers, provoking almost a primeval response in them, a kind of bodily knowing as they come into close contact with such exhibits. Such creations bring us face to face with the fact that we are all participants as well as victims in such acts of violence.

A taxidermist often requires a clay model that serves as a guiding structure for the real mount. Robert Bloch's novel, *Psycho*, is the clay model on which Hitchcock's film is based. Bloch shows Norman as a fat, shy man in his forties. We first encounter him reading a description of the Aztec victory dance in *The Realm of the Incas* which describes how the enemy, after being defeated, is killed and his whole body is transformed into a "sound box":

The drumbeat for this was usually performed on what had been the body of an enemy: the skin had been flayed and the belly stretched to form a drum, and the whole body acted as a sound box while throbbings came out of the open mouth—grotesque, but effective.

(Bloch 2014, 1–2)

With a "comfortable shiver" Norman then indulges in his fantasy, "[I]magine flaying a man—alive, probably—and then stretching his belly to use it as a drum! How did they actually go about doing that, curing and preserving the flesh of the corpse to prevent decay?" (Bloch 1959, 2) Such descriptions of rendering a body permanently motionless, mutilating it, and then transforming it into a replica of itself, only more compliant this time, bring the basic idea of taxidermy to mind.[3]

Hitchcock, however, is doing far more than being merely faithful to the plot of the original novel. Bloch treats Mary's (Marion in *Psycho*) murder with much economy—a description that arouses fear but fails somehow to arouse our empathy for the victim:

> The roar [of the shower] was deafening, and the room was beginning to steam up. That's why she didn't hear the door open, or note the sound of footsteps. And at first, when the shower curtains parted, the steam obscured the face. Then she *did* see it there—just a face, peering through the curtains, hanging in midair like a mask. A head-scarf concealed the hair and the glassy eyes stared inhumanly, but it wasn't a mask, it couldn't be. The skin had been powdered dead—white and two hectic spots of rouge centred on the cheekbones. It wasn't a mask. It was the face of a crazy old woman. *Mary started to scream, and then the curtains parted further and a hand appeared, holding a butcher's knife. It was the knife that, a moment later, cut off her scream. And her head.*
>
> (1959, 24–5)

Alfred Hitchcock creates one of the most blood-curdling and yet one of the most pathetic scenes in film history out of those above-quoted last thirty-three words of Bloch's novel.

---

[3] Bloch further elaborates on how the dead scream of a corpse is used as the siren of a victor's triumph: "the old crone crouching before them, throbbing out a relentless rhythm on the swollen, distended belly of a cadaver. The contorted mouth of the corpse would be forced open … and from it the sound emerged. Beating from the belly, rising through the shrunken inner orifices, forced up through the withered windpipe to emerge amplified and in full force from the dead throat" (Bloch 2014, 2).

After the murder in *Psycho* (unlike the novel which switches abruptly to Norman waking from a stupor in his room), Hitchcock's camera lingers in the bathroom, exploring the aftermath of the violence. Its focus on the shower head, Marion's legs in the tub, the course of the blood that flows toward the drain, her face pressed against the toilet floor, and her eyes staring back at us, serve to complicate our emotions: a mixture of horror, disbelief, and shame. The vulnerability and helplessness of a body bereft of life and open to the stark gaze of the viewer bring forth the uneasy sensation of our lust for dreadful sights thinly disguised under a mask of shocked sympathy. The tight close shots of Marion's naked corpse and the camera's roving around the site of the massacre, though visually comprehensible are yet perplexing to classify. Such perplexity probably arises from wondering as to what is more shocking, "the human violence … or the idea that someone was transform[ing] these vestiges into something else" (Milgrom 2010, 3). While on a fourteen-day trek "through the most barren stretch of Tanzania," Melissa Milgrom meets a group of Belgian hunters and in their camp, she comes across an array of animal skin:

> I mistakenly wandered into the carcass room, where the hunters stored their kills. The salted pelts, hung high on pegs, were eyeless, mangled, and limp. They smelled bloody and metallic: the unmistakable stench of decay. I wasn't sure what was more shocking: the human violence after all the tranquility or the idea that someone was going to transform these vestiges into something else.
>
> (2010, 3)

She later adds, "[T]here's something arresting and haunting" as well as "something morbid and kitschy about taxidermy" (2010, 6). Just the kind of adjectives that can be applied to the shower scene. We may visualize Hitchcock using a "torso," a "body double," the "hands," "shoulders," and "head" of Janet Leigh as raw materials out of which he fleshes out one of the most effective slashings.

While Norma Bates is a corpse that is re-animated, Marion offers us a reverse narrative of the body. She embodies the presence of death within life even before she dies on-screen. The use of another body as her substitute before her murder in the shower scene, the dispassionate, almost clinical considerations of how her body shall be strategically used in the murder scene reduces her to an object that is merely acted upon. Just as Judy Barton's body in *Vertigo* becomes a living tomb of at least two dead women—Carlotta Valdes and Madeleine Elster; death also resides in the live body of Marion as her body is molded and replaced at times to fit the demands of the kill-scene: a passive body, as Laura Mulvey would say, to be actively gazed on.

Death is a precondition in the art of taxidermy. Samuel J. M. M. Alberti in *The Afterlives of Animals* states, "the biological death of the living beast is the birth of the specimen" (2011, 14). Norma Bates had to be killed to be preserved. But in the case of Marion, Hitchcock reverses the process. Marion becomes a specimen, an object whose body is used as raw material to create the infamous slashing scene even before she dies. Helen Gregory and Anthony Purdy in "Present Signs, Dead Things: Indexical Authenticity and Taxidermy's Nonabsent Animal" (2015), while attempting a parallel between photography and taxidermy, speak of the current trends in taxidermy. They state that "artists have shifted away from addressing issues surrounding representations or simulacra of life as portrayed through a dead specimen and moved toward the creation of sculpture that frequently relies for its impact upon a self-conscious depiction of its own deadness" (Gregory and Purdy 2015, 74–5). They describe Emily Mayer's sculpture, *Last Resting Place (Their Death in My Hands)* (2007) in the following manner:

> It depicts a dead cat resting on a taxidermist's workbench alongside tools, sketches, and a mug filled with pens and pencils and functions as a commentary on mortality and on the pet as a site of embodied memories. In this case, the cat does not appear to be sleeping; it is evidently and uncompromisingly dead, waiting for the taxidermist to perform her magic.
>
> (Gregory and Purdy 2015, 75)

The shower scene in *Psycho* where Hitchcock "creates" the most operative slashing (one that has been, and is still being, recreated again and again) may be interpreted as an anticipation of the installation that Gregory and Purdy speak of. The only difference is that the task of recreation begins way before the "exhibit" is dead. It is Janet Leigh's (the real woman who plays Marion) "head," "shoulder," and "legs" that are being used while the "torso" is that of another model (Marli Renfro), as stated by Hitchcock (*Hitchcock/Truffaut* 1984, 277). The dismemberment is carried out on a live body on screen.

The title of Mayer's sculpture/installation "Their Death in my Hands" acquires a sinister tone when applied to Hitchcock's staging of violence on the female body. The shower head, the tub, the drain, the curtains, and the cold white walls call to mind "a taxidermist's workbench alongside tools, sketches, and a mug filled with pens and pencils." The dead eye of Marion, her face pressed on the bathroom floor, becomes a "commentary on mortality," the randomness of violence, and a site of wasted hopes. One significant point of departure is that, unlike the cat, Marion is not "waiting for the taxidermist to perform [his or] her magic"; the magic is generated in the very process of dying. It is the enactment of pain and torture that Hitchcock preserves. Hitchcock knows that the compelling effect of the scene on the viewer would depend upon a foregrounding of the unmistakable "deadness" of the desecrated body, and all the props in the bathroom so meticulously recorded shall add to the horror of this taxidermal installation.

Gloom and Gore: From Noir to Slasher

Direct physical torture meted out to a female body and its explicit presentation on screen was not a regular feature in mainstream Hollywood films. It was *Psycho* and its notorious shower scene that initiated a trend of vivid torture of female bodies in Hollywood. It may be argued that earlier strict censorship codes prevented the filming of such scenes. But despite the relative relaxation of the Hays Code, Hitchcock had to overcome several obstacles in his efforts of making *Psycho*.[4] Paramount was doubtful about the script because of its overt sexual content and vivid physical violence. Hitchcock's decision

---

[4] See "Hitchcock and the Hollywood Production Code" by Maria Del Carmen Garrido Hornos for a history of the Motion Picture Production Code. The essay gives us a detailed account of Hitchcock's constant interactions with the "Code functionaries" in the pre-production stage of *Psycho* and the way he overcomes the hurdles imposed by a studio system that was not willing to permit a film with such blatant exhibition of sex and violence, and ultimately succeeds in obtaining a "B" [which means "morally objectionable in part for all"] from the Catholic League of Decency for the film (*Peeping through the Holes*, ed. by Garrido Hornos 2013, 1–22).

to use his television crew and the cheap settings of his television series at Universal Studios for *Psycho* may be traced to Paramount's hesitation to be a wholehearted participant in this project. The non-cooperation of the Studio, the skeptical attitude of contemporary critics who found the plot to be too trivial, and an audience who were already over-stuffed by a daily dose of adventure and violence dished out at their very homes every day by the television soaps, *Psycho*, one could expect, was bound to fail. Despite so many odds, Hitchcock went ahead with his project. He decided to finance a major part of the project with Paramount having a forty percent stake (Durgnat 2002, 12–14). *Psycho* not only succeeded, but it also grossed over three times its production cost and made Hitchcock one of the richest and one of the most powerful filmmakers of the time.

The success of *Psycho* may partly be traced to the ambivalence it creates in the audience's mind regarding a woman's body and her sexuality. *Psycho* was introduced to a world that had been witness to two World Wars, the Holocaust, and the stifling atmosphere of the Cold War. Society was already composed of skeptical and pessimistic individuals who were petrified, anxious, and lonely. Hollywood, the guardian of popular American imagination imposed strict codes to manufacture films that had no place for blatant exhibition of instincts like sex and violence. This world of entertainment had to adhere to a make-believe world that would somehow manage to wipe off the bitter memories of systematic cruelty hurled from time to time on human bodies and minds. It also helped in assuaging the guilt of a nation that had not been involved enough until it was too late. In such a world came *Psycho* with a woman in her undergarments, a woman who spells out the word "bathroom," and a woman who is mercilessly slashed on-screen, a slashing that was unprecedented in the history of Hollywood. There was murder, there was blood, there was violence, and there was sex.

Psycho must also be situated within the context of the sociocultural crisis caused by the sexual revolution of the late 1950s and early 1960s as well as the Second Wave Feminism. Postwar America was not a congenial space for women's sexual freedom. It was a time when the values of family and proper respectable living were being endorsed with great enthusiasm. The rise of the noir films in the 1940s and 1950s brought in its wake numerous instances of the threats posed by femme fatales to the integrity of heteronormative families: a femme fatale who transgresses the boundaries prescribed for women and poses a threat to the security of familial and societal bonds, but is ultimately tamed to the relief of conventional patriarchy. The films would inevitably end with a familiar scene of a humiliated and humbled woman, either begging for mercy or taking recourse to self-annihilation out of sheer remorse, an end well-deserved, much to the joy of a triumphant and relieved audience. John Huston's *The Maltese Falcon* (1941), Billy Wilder's *Double Indemnity* (1944), *The Lost Weekend* (1945), and *Sunset Boulevard* (1950), Howard Hawks' *The Big Sleep* (1946), Jacques Tourneur's *Out of the Past* (1947), Otto Preminger's *Laura* (1944), Edward Dmytryk's *Murder, My Sweet* (1944), Fritz Lang's *The Big Heat* (1953), Tay Garnett's *The Postman Always Rings Twice* (1946), Orson Welles' *The Lady from Shanghai* (1947) and *Touch of Evil* (1958), Robert Aldrich's *Kiss Me Deadly* (1955), and numerous other noirs—in style, mood, perspective, and tone—flooded Hollywood from 1940s and reached their peak in the 1950s. Such films with all their gloom and postwar anxiety were always alert in reminding the audience of the damaging effect that a female transgressor may have on the structure of a family, the building block of a society.

E. Ann Kaplan in her introduction to *Women in Film Noir* (1980) stresses the changing role of women in the film noir under the thriller genre. Unlike the conventional thrillers where women are confined within the domestic space and serve as backgrounds to the ideological task of the film that is completed by the men, "[t]he *film noir world* is one in which women are central to the intrigue of the films ... Defined by their sexuality, which is presented as desirable but dangerous to men, the women function as the obstacle to the male quest" (Kaplan 1980, 3).[5] The hero's success or failure depends on whether he can escape the "tentacles" of a woman's "snare." Usually, the entire film ultimately seems to be a project designed to tame,

---

[5] *Women in Film Noir* (1980) is a collection of eight essays that attempts to read the world of Film Noir through feminist film theory that assesses the position of women in postwar crisis. The essays attempt either to tease out a progressive analysis of an apparently regressive film or attempt an incisive reading of a supposedly progressive film with hidden sexist agenda, thereby vesting the noir films with potentials of both progressive and regressive dimensions.

contain and destroy the aberrant female and her sexuality. Sylvia Harvey in "Woman's Place: the absent family of film noir" in *Women in Film Noir* traces the cause of female suppression in noir films to a churning in family relations (1980, 22–34). Family as an institution was losing its place of consecration. There was an abrupt change in the professional space of the nation as well. Women who had become a large section of the workforce during the war were suddenly quitting the job market after the war to cater to the demands of war veterans back home. Thus, female sexuality, a direct consequence of female economic and social independence, had to be curbed and placed in the "proper" hierarchical order.

It was in such an atmosphere of rigid conformity that Marilyn Monroe emerged and was hailed as the greatest postwar sex symbol. Her films like *Niagara* (1953), *Gentlemen Prefer Blondes* (1953), *How to Marry a Millionaire* (1953), *The Seven Year Itch* (1955), and *Some Like It Hot* (1959) were films that not only made her a sex icon but also brought forth a lady who was extremely comfortable in her skin. Her nude sessions with photographer Tom Kelly in 1949 became sensational news. One of her nude photos was subsequently published by Hugh Hefner in the first issue of Playboy in 1953, and Monroe was hailed as the first "Playmate of the Month." Hefner has been reported saying: "She was the most in control when she was in the nude. What would be a position of vulnerability for others was a position of power for her" (quoted by Olivia Barker 2012). Another major challenge was the popularity of Hugh Hefner's *Playboy* (1953). It not only interrogated every aspect of conventional sexuality, but one of the professed agendas of the magazine was to free nudity from the stain of lewdness. The first edition of *Playboy* sold 54,175 copies at 50 cents each. America was waking up to a new revolution. Discourses on female sexuality were gradually occupying center stage on the social and political front.

The 1960s were a time of major social upheaval with a restructuring of gender relations. The postwar crisis and the rise of the welfare state altered the traditional social functions of men and women. Women entered the professional world and became financially more self-reliant. Consequently, changes were also felt in the domestic sphere as women gained more control over their lives. Karl Djerassi invented the first reliable contraceptive pills in 1960 which implied that women could now have more control over their bodies. This separation of sexual intercourse from the purpose of procreation significantly altered both male and female sexuality. As terms like "love" and "sex" acquired new implications, they altered the entire space of the body. Moreover, the counter-cultural social movements of the 1960s—the students' movement across Europe and the anti-war movements—advocated greater sexual freedom. In their attempt to subvert authoritarian states based on capitalist ideologies, they protested against any form of repression that curbs natural urges.

Prominent social thinkers like Herbert Marcuse, Erich Fromm, and Wilhelm Reich, projected repression of sexuality as a deliberate ploy of bourgeois capitalism and liberated "sex" from the stigmas of "abnormality," "disease," and "moral depravity." Sex was considered healthy, positive, and natural. Reich states that it is the suppression of instincts by all forms of cultural institutions which work as handmaiden of capitalism that is responsible for an individual's "neurosis" (*The Sexual Revolution* 1986, 8). Reich calls for a "sexual revolution" that would liberate all forms of sexual identities from the fetters of patriarchal and capitalist repression.

It was amidst such turbulence of the 1950s and 1960s that Hitchcock creates some of the major and some of the most controversial films of his life—*Vertigo* (1958), *Psycho* (1960), *The Birds* (1963), *Marnie* (1964), and *Frenzy* (1972). Hitchcock's *Psycho* and its shower murder shocked contemporary audiences with its blatant depiction of the brutal stabbing of a female body. It has been widely considered a film that spurred the genre of exploitation/slasher films that fed on sexual titillation and gore during the late 1960s and 1970s. Any reference to *Psycho* brings to mind the images of Marion Crane being hacked to death with water streaming down her screaming body. The scene is so famous that even the ones who have not watched the film are aware of it. Further, Bernard Herrmann's jagged, discordant music has been used in numerous other films as an ominous harbinger of a "psycho." Hitchcock may thus be situated at the crux of a filmic continuum as he plays the pivotal role of converting the more restrained version of "educating" and "taming" deviant female bodies in the film noirs of the 1940s and 1950s to an all-out slashing of a female body (perhaps, as a reaction to the new waves of sexual revolution in contemporary America) that spurred on the slashers of the 1960s and the 1970s.

Psycho had cost 800,000 dollars to make and had grossed more than fifteen million dollars at the time (*Hitchcock/Truffaut* 1984, 283). It was Hitchcock's greatest success and Hollywood immediately pricked its ears to its success. Carol J. Clover in *Men Women and Chain Saws* (1993) notes: "Where once there was one victim, Marion Crane, there are now many: five in *Texas Chain Saw I*, four in *Halloween*, fourteen in *Friday the Thirteenth III*, and so on" (32). And William Schoell, in *Stay Out of the Shower* (1985), points out the reason for such a proliferation: "other filmmakers figured that the only thing better than one beautiful woman being gruesomely murdered was a whole series of beautiful women being gruesomely murdered" (35). Herschell Gordon Lewis' *Blood Feast* (1963), Tobe Hooper's *Chainsaw Massacre* (1974), and John Carpenter's *Halloween* (1978) all proved to be extremely successful. The film *Halloween* broke all previous box office records, not only of other horror films but also of any type of films made by independent production houses of the time.

Horror and pornography are the two genres that specifically thrive on the arousal of bodily sensations. Slashers have imbibed elements of both these genres. Adding sex with gore is the easiest way to woo the viewers. The basic premise of taxidermy, which is, how to mold a body into a compliant exhibit for the satiation of human curiosity and human longing, finds an unmistakable parallel in these horror films. That these same exhibits generate a counter-narrative furthers the analogy between these two genres centered on corporeality. Alfred Hitchcock, by adapting Bloch's novel on-screen plays a crucial role in ushering the application of this corporeal art in mainstream cinema. Taxidermy with all its anthropocentric connotations and subjective mutations finds a natural abode in the desolate world of a roadside motel owner.

"Dress Down to Be Killed": Slashers and Skin Shows

In a slasher, often a female character's lack of "proper clothes" becomes pronounced at the climactic point of murder. In cinema, as the saying goes, "women dress down to be killed." In *Psycho*, Marion is shown in her undergarments on more than one occasion, and, in keeping with the sex/slaughter formula, we get glimpses of her flesh (most of which belong to a body double) in the shower scene. Hitchcock here combines scopophilia with gratuitous gore—almost luring the audience to male gaze their way into the entire process of murder. Thus, it may seem that *Psycho* contributes to producing films that deliberately sexualize slaughter. The censure that the genre faces for portraying vicious attacks against women mostly, and for mixing sex scenes with violent acts may also be directed at *Psycho*. The shower scene with its glimpse of the female body does not equate itself to an all-out sex scene, but it is definitely intentional as every aspect of the character's femininity is carefully and meticulously fashioned in this scene.

However, Hitchcock's severe editing technique in the scene shifts our focus from titillation to horror. James Monaco, in *How to Read a Film* (2009), states, "[s]eventy separate shots in less than a minute of screen time are fused together psychologically into a continuous experience: a frightening and graphic knife attack" (196–7). Much is left to the imagination as we go frame by frame through the entire scene. We see a knife, blood, water, and a woman's naked body (with certain parts strategically concealed from the camera). Unlike the typical slasher films, there are no gashes in *Psycho*. We find blood, but it is not a gore feast. We can see Marion screaming, but the scream is almost drowned as the slashing chords of Bernard Hermann's soundtrack make up for a far more gruesome sound effect. The closing shots are profoundly tragic, as blood and water swirl down the drain, the camera cuts to a close shot of the gaping drain, and dissolves into Marion's eyeball. The shock is not only due to the suddenness of the murder or the explosion of cuts on screen, but also the fact that Hitchcock has killed off his leading lady with more than an hour left of the film. Robert Bloch's novel *Psycho*, on which the film is based, opens with Norman Bates and goes on with the tedious details of his life before we are introduced to Mary. The film, as a significant departure from the novel, opens with Marion. Till the murder of Marion, we see the film through her eyes. Hitchcock mostly uses eye-line matching shots so that the viewers see the drama unfold through her eyes. Hitchcock even makes her share her thoughts with us and makes us feel what she feels only to see her naked body hacked to an ugly death. *Psycho*, despite inspiring slashers, conveys that there is more to a kill scene than the skin of a shirtless woman.

"Avoid Sex": Sex and Slaughter

In *Horror Movie Freak* (2010), Don Sumner states the rules of survival in a horror film. The first rule is: "Avoid sex. Sex is equal to death" (12). This is especially applicable to women. A promiscuous woman is a more likely candidate for a brutal murder. *Psycho* is guilty of this sexism. The film begins in a typical Hitchcockian fashion as the camera pans through a large city (Phoenix, Arizona). The date is Friday, December 11, and the time is 2.43 pm. The camera then seems to search and choose a random window from among numerous buildings and enters the zone of the personal. The opening almost seems like an on-screen rendition of a newspaper report, with place, date, and time stated, moving toward a voyeuristic peep into an individual's private space. We get our first glimpse of the supposed main character. She is a blonde, a Hitchcock trademark, and she is in her undergarments sharing a post-coital space with her secret lover. Their conversation makes it clear that the lovers are unable to marry for financial constraints. She has committed the "sin" of fornication, and, therefore, must be "punished." The film may be seen as pairing violence and sexuality in a fetishist binary, like the later slasher films.

Tania Modleski, in *The Women Who Knew Too Much* (2005), points out that in *Psycho* Marion Crane is identified with various forms of "filth." The film constantly associates her with "money ('filthy lucre'), bathrooms, toilets, blood, and, of course, the swamp" (109). Modleski further states that not only are the women objects of the male gaze, but they are also recipients of most of the punishment in the film. After the death of Marion Crane in the shower, the camera focuses on her sightless eye. When Norman Bates' mother's corpse is finally revealed, it is Marion's sister who is forced to confront the horrible spectacle; while she screams, the swinging light bulb is reflected in the eye sockets of the mother's corpse and, finally, at the end of the film, when Norman has completely lost himself in his mother, his mother (through her son's body) is agonizingly aware of being stared at and tries desperately to demonstrate her harmlessness to her unseen but ever present observers by proclaiming that she cannot even swat a fly. Modleski emphasizes in her book that her purpose is to "defend that much maligned woman, Mrs. Bates, whose male child suffers such a severe 'overidentification' with her that he is driven to matricide and the rape/murder of various young women." She goes on to state, "At the end of the film, 'Mrs. Bates' (who has the last word) speaks through her son's body to protest her innocence and place the blame for the crimes against women on her son. I think she speaks the truth" (Modleski 2005, 14).

But a comparison of the novel with the film reveals that Hitchcock's *Psycho* is way more invested in Marion than Bloch's *Psycho* is in Mary. A close reading of the shower scene shows how the audience, along with Marion, goes through this entire process of pain and horror. The argument that Hitchcock punishes Marion for her untamed sexuality is somehow eclipsed by our sense of shock, pain, and shame—the uneasy realization of being a voyeur. The dead, and the mutilated are, after all, at such a disadvantage and Hitchcock makes us suffer with the dead, with the mutilated. This, however, does not mean that Hitchcock was largely sympathetic toward women in his films. Post-*Psycho*, his films become increasingly ruthless toward women. And his penultimate film, *Frenzy* (1972), is a fitting climax to the filmmaker's filming of fear through tortured female bodies littering the city he was born in.

Live Signs on Dead Skin: *Frenzy*

In *The Modernist Corpse* (2018), Erin E. Edwards speaks of how a dead body has the capacity to weave a narrative around it. It is called "corpse-power ... that moves and shapes the living world" (6). A corpse signifies the termination of a rationalist regulation of the body. It becomes a site where its cultural and social identity is overtaken by purely biological factors. However, narratives of brutalized, tortured, dismembered, and murdered bodies carry forward the remnants of the person "once-alive" even after the molecular procedures of putrefaction work their way in. The narrative of murder mysteries lends a dead body a "life" of its own. It is in this genre that the posthumous travels along with the living.

In 1972, Alfred Hitchcock's *Frenzy* is released. It is a police procedural where a serial killer is tracked through a careful study of female corpses. The setting, accessories, clothes, and marks on the female victims are analyzed to eke out clues that would lead to the murderer. The corpses of Brenda and Babs, the two most prominent female victims of *Frenzy*, show how voyeurism and sadism inform the representation of an immobile naked female body under the garb of a police procedural. In *Frenzy*, the skin of a dead woman is both a site of forensic investigation and voyeurism. It acts as a cipher to be decoded—medically and sexually. The post-murder masculinist investigative gaze forces a kind of mock life on these victims through the relentless search for a killer's live signs on their dead flesh.

Frenzy depicts a modern dystopic London where a serial killer is at large and the police are clueless apart from the fact that the killer strangles his victim with a tie after raping her. The protagonist of the film, Robert Blaney (Jon Finch), is shown as an impatient man given to sudden outbursts of temper. He has lost his job, is divorced, and is going through the lowest phase of his life. Circumstances prove more fatal for him as the plot progresses and he is accused of killing his ex-wife Brenda (Barbara Leigh-Hunt) and is suspected of being the much sought-after serial killer. However, the audience knows that it is his friend, Robert Rusk (Barry Foster) who is the real murderer. Rusk also rapes and murders Blaney's lover Babs Milligan (Anna Massey) and frames Blaney for the murder and gets him arrested. The chief inspector, Oxford (Alec McCowen), who is in charge of the case, is not satisfied with the verdict and investigates further. He gets some incriminating evidence against Rusk: clues relating to Babs' murder. In the meantime, Blaney escapes from the prison hospital and reaches Rusk's apartment to kill him, only to discover another dead woman on his bed. Inspector Oxford also reaches Rusk's apartment at the same time and catches Rusk in the act of bringing in a large box, meant as a coffin for the victim.

It was twelve years after *Psycho* that Hitchcock came up with another film that indulged in a direct display of naked dead female bodies on-screen. In *Frenzy*, much in the vein of *Psycho*, the brutal exhibition of female corpses shows us a world where bodies are not spared even after death. However, while *Psycho* is chiefly concerned with the concealing of corpses, *Frenzy* is about displaying them.

Frenzy was released at a time when slasher films were at full sway. *Frenzy* is a combination of titillation and violence in keeping with the spirit of the slashers. But based on serial killing and police procedural, it also combines voyeurism with surveillance by focusing on the juridical system that situates the bodies of the victims within the discourse of material scrutiny. The vandalized bodies that are so casually dismissed in the film and yet shown with such meticulous clarity serve as early instances of many such bodies to come in twentieth and twenty-first-century films that are decoded by forensic science and pathology. Such bodies seem to become tired spaces where this endless conflict of gaining control is carried out through the systematic processes of watching, knowing, and then taming.

Hitchcock's London

Hitchcock made twenty-three films in Britain before moving to America in 1939. But he never could leave his city as many of his Hollywood films were shot in London. From the chase through the British Museum in *Blackmail* (1929) to the Royal Albert Hall set-piece in *The Man Who Knew Too Much* (1956), he contributed significantly to the myth of London. Hitchcock's first critically acclaimed work was *The Lodger* made in 1927 and his last major success was *Frenzy* made in 1972. Both films have London as their setting. The city as projected in *The Lodger* (1927) has traveled a long way to become what it has in *Frenzy*. In *The Lodger*, we find traces of a Victorian urban space, a city made infamous by serial killers such as Jack the Ripper and Sweeney Todd, a place where Dorian Gray roamed the murky streets of crime and squalor and a place where Mr. Hyde went on a rampage in dark alleys when the city slept. Hitchcock may be seen as a flaneur of these alleys.

The Lodger reminds us of a Dickensian London, while London in *Frenzy* is a city of blackened buildings and long-vanished alleyways, a city that is changing rapidly. *Frenzy* depicts a modern dystopic London where a serial killer is on rampage. The violence, the grotesqueness of the bodies, the dispassionate account of the murders discussed in bars, public gatherings, and private dinners, and the superabundance of food and drink, all project an obese city, trapped in its consumptive indulgence. London in Hitchcock's films journeys from the noir world of remorse as projected in *The Lodger* of the 1920s to a metropolis of remorseless cruelty in *Frenzy* of the 1970s. From the fog in the night streets of London in *The Lodger* to the flourish of the first shot in *Frenzy* that shows a majestic London with its Tower Bridge glittering in sunshine and to the swooping down of the camera and focusing on a woman's body floating on the Thames, one can find markers of the evolution of Hitchcock's way of representing violence.

Edible Commodity/Inedible Pollutant

The whole corpus of *Frenzy* may be seen as a display of grotesqueness. Hitchcock chooses to bring out that grotesqueness through dead bodies of women and images of nauseating meals. In Hitchcock's *Shadow of a Doubt* (1943) Uncle Charlie in a dinner table conversation derides the world as a "foul sty" and equates the "lazy" widows of the world to "fat pigs" wallowing in filthy lucre. In *Psycho*, Marion is consistently associated with filth after she steals 40,000 dollars. She is linked to dirty money, washrooms, blood, and finally a swamp where her body is sucked in. This connection is continued in *Frenzy* where women are associated with food and filth. The film opens with a politician's promise of cleansing the river of "pollution" and "waste products" precisely at a moment when a naked tie-strangled body of an anonymous woman floats down the water of Thames. The association is clearly stated at the very outset. The corpse is gross and it serves as a source of visual pollution in a perfect setting of a sunny London day, adding to the filth in the Thames.

The four dead women and their bodies that become objects of disgust for some, and pity for others, seem grotesque at least in the ambivalence that they stir in us through their blunt visibility. Applying Levi-Strauss' study of myths where women are seen as "both edible commodity and inedible pollutant" (Modleski 2005, 107), Tania Modleski attempts a reading of *Frenzy* that stresses Hitchcock's ambivalence to femininity: "In *Frenzy*, ambivalence can be related to the polarity woman as food vs. woman as poison" (2005, 107). *Frenzy* is replete with instances where women are unabashedly compared to objects that can be tasted and ingested: Rusk's false assurance to Brenda just before he rapes and kills her ("There's a saying in the fruit business ... don't squeeze the goods until they're yours"), his partaking of Brenda's apple before and after he rapes and kills her (thus treating the apple as an entrée and dessert), the stuffing of Babs in a potato truck, the effort that Inspector Oxford gives in cutting the meat on his plate with his knife and fork (see Figure 4.2) replicated in the immediate next scene where Rusk tries to prise open Babs' dead stiff fingers with the small knife of his nail cutter to retrieve his tiepin (see Figure 4.3), the stiff body of Babs lying on the road reminding us of the grotesque-looking pig's trotter (see Figure 4.4) that Inspector Oxford tries to gulp down while narrating the crime against Brenda at dinner table, and finally the reference to the breaking of Babs' fingers at a time when Oxford's wife snaps breadsticks and munches them are clear indications of what the film is doing. It is equating tortured dead female corpses to dead meat that Oxford's wife forces on him.

Figure 4.2 Oxford trying to cut a piece of meat, *Frenzy*.

Figure 4.3 Rusk trying to prise open Bab's stiff fingers, *Frenzy*.

Figure 4.4 Bab's body on the road resembles the pig's trotter on Oxford's plate, *Frenzy*.

Human Beauty and Bestial Fear

Hitchcock in *Frenzy* is doing exactly the opposite of what Brooklyn-based taxidermist Kate Clark does today. While Hitchcock takes a perfectly "normal" body and transforms it into a grotesque specimen, Clark takes a dead, damaged, nonhuman hide and attempts to transform it into something beautiful and appealing. She sculpts human face (made of clay) on a conventional taxidermy mount. She etches and wraps carefully crafted human features on the skin of the nonhuman corpse. She takes damaged hides and "repurposes" them to give an added layer of meaning to her artwork. Clark explains, "the human face changes the hierarchy ... I have a model sit and freehand sculpt the face and [put] the leather on it." She does not intend to make the mount "monstery," as she desires to maintain "a balance between it being really appealing and something familiar and also being really unfamiliar" (Clark 2015, 4:2). In a few words Clark precisely brings home the paradox inherent in every taxidermied mount—a sense of the uncanny. An otherwise grotesque sight of a flayed skin gradually gets the shape of an animal body with the face of a beautiful human being, bringing together the "familiar" and the "unfamiliar."

On the other hand, grotesqueness is etched upon a conventional female anatomy right before the viewers in *Frenzy* through vivid depictions of rape, murder, dismemberment, and a casual dismissal of helpless victims who become ridiculous shadows of their former bodies with their eyes bulging out, their tongues sticking out and their legs jutting out. While Clark admits that "it can be unnerving to have the human face staring back," hence she tries to soothe the viewers by constructing the eyes as the most "beautiful part of the face—the lids with the animal's real lashes," (see Figure 4.5) in *Frenzy*, it is Brenda's and Babs' eyes bulging out straight at us which ironically are the most disconcerting feature of their faces after death (see Figure 4.6).

The near-naked Brenda, the completely naked rigid corpse of Babs, and the woman floating down the Thames are transformed, through these imposed "grotesque guises," into bodies of display. Both the dead antelope and the dead women become meeting grounds for the human and the nonhuman. While the sculptor of one wants to make the mount palatable by bestowing it with beautiful eyes and soft eyelashes, the other successfully transmutes beautiful bodies into outrageous exhibits with raw animal fear etched on their dead faces.

It is through the construction and propagation of a fixed idea of a "normative" body that patriarchy holds sway, and it is through the destruction of this constructed normative body that patriarchy threatens to devalue the female body. As Xavier Aldana Reyes suggests, the "structures of biopolitics

Figure 4.5 Kate Clark's "Licking the Plate". Taxidermied antelope with a human face. Courtesy Kate Clark.

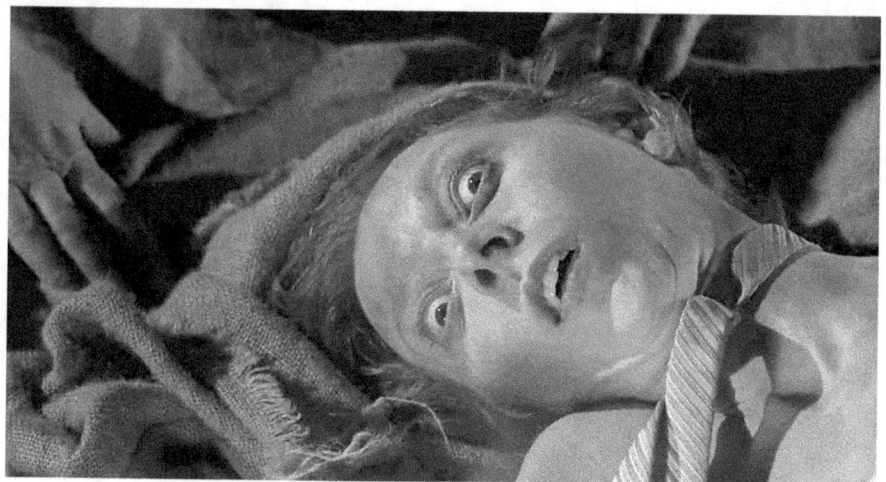

Figure 4.6 Bab's dead face staring back at us, *Frenzy*.

or advertising" (2014, 7) create the yardsticks of the normal and the indexes for the "lingering shadow of the abnormal, the freak, the grotesque" (Edwards and Graulund 2013, 86). Grotesquery itself becomes a weapon in the hands of patriarchy that threatens to destabilize the paradigm of a "normative" female physiognomy through the tools of ridicule or revulsion.

As an added layer of humiliation, to further the idea of a grotesque face, Hitchcock had planned to show saliva dripping from Brenda's mouth (Spoto 1999, 546). Such an attempt at degrading a body beyond life reminds us of Mary Douglas' idea of defilement that she connects with margins of the body in *Purity and Danger* (1966):

> all margins are dangerous. If they are pulled this way or that the shape of fundamental experience is altered. Any structure of ideas is vulnerable at its margins. We should expect the orifices of the body to symbolise its specially vulnerable points. Matter issuing from them is marginal stuff of the most obvious kind. Spittle, blood, milk, urine, faeces or tears by simply issuing forth have traversed the boundary of the body.
>
> (2003, 122)

A woman's body is read as a source of pollution in *Frenzy*, and a dead woman's body more so. It is the ultimate embodiment of nauseating filth.

In keeping with the parallel between speciesism and sexism, and drawing on Mary Douglas' ideas of purity and defilement, Julia Kristeva in *Powers of Horror* (1982) states: "Impure animals become even more impure once they are dead ... contact with their carcasses must be avoided" (109). It is ironical that the "carcasses" of these "impure" female characters need to be visited and revisited throughout the film: by the investigators to dig out clues to the murders, by the murderer to erase his traces (his tiepin) on the body, and by the respectable citizens of London in their untiring analysis of the corpses at pubs, public gatherings, and dinner tables. Investigation, scrutiny, surveillance, and the constant rummaging of the corpses smudge the "boundary" between the "pollutant" and the "pure," forcing investigators, the sexual psychopath, and curious bystanders to participate in these rites of defilement.

Sloppy Crimes and Malleable Bodies

In the recent past, there has been a proliferation of forensic detective novels and films where the role of the forensic pathologist becomes crucial to discover and analyze traces on/in the body of the dead that can shed light on the causes of death and the identity of the perpetrator. Shorn of conventional forms of agency, the corpse nevertheless becomes the primary actant that helps revisit and reconstruct the crime scene around it. In crime narratives, surveillance of the corpse remains a primary method of crime detection. The body not only carries with it the anatomical remnants of a life history but also material hints of the body of the perpetrator, hints that must be brought out through careful rummaging and meticulous scrutiny of the deceased. It is through constant handling and examining of the dead body that the categories and attributes of the once live body are reinscribed in death. What we witness is a close surveillance of a medicalized body through the meticulous use of forensic technologies. The body becomes a space to be delved into for clues of the perpetrator's corporeal remnants such as hair, semen, and blood.

Frenzy is one of the few films of Hitchcock's that deal with serial killing. Also, while the previous films take recourse to witnesses, alibis, circumstantial evidence, and careful scrutiny of settings, *Frenzy* frequently speaks of examining the dead body through which traces of the killer can be found (for instance, scrutiny of the clothes of the deceased, the marks of strangulation on Brenda's neck, the face powder on Blaney's money and the potato dust on Babs' body later found on Rusk's clothes). However, Hitchcock chooses to undermine forensic science. *Frenzy* is a sloppy crime story with a careless killer, a wronged man with whom we do not sympathize, and a detective clearly more distressed by his wife's culinary skills than the ever-increasing number of female corpses littered throughout London. There are numerous loopholes in the plot: the ties with which the women are murdered have fingerprints of the killer that are not matched with Blaney's fingerprints, the alibis are not checked properly, and the fact that a crime is committed at a time when Blaney is in jail that would naturally exonerate him from his guilt is not given much thought. We may conclude that *Frenzy* as a detective story fails precisely because the filmmaker is not much concerned with the technicalities of crime detection. *Frenzy* is a crime film that is more concerned with the staging of naked dead women. The film stands more on the shock induced by the ravaged bodies than on the tracking and punishing of the perpetrator.

Frenzy is the only film where Hitchcock relentlessly stages a prolonged rape and murder scene where there is no calculated positioning of the camera to hide the violence (as in *Blackmail*,[6] *Strangers on a Train*,[7] and *Psycho*) that can

---

[6] In *Blackmail* the struggle between Alice White (Annie Ondra) and the obsessed artist (Cyril Ritchard) is not shown directly. Just as the tension between the characters rise, the camera cuts to a long shot of a police patrolling the streets. The next shot takes us back into the room and focuses on a wall that is half-obscured with darkness where the shadows of two struggling figures appear. The wall itself functions as a screen on which we witness a play of shadows. We are twice removed from the action as we watch a struggle on screen that gets reflected on another screen, a wall that is half veiled in darkness. From a medium static shot of the wall, the camera gradually moves from left to right. We now expect to see the struggle directly without the medium of the wall. But our expectation is thwarted as we are confronted with another screen, the screen of a curtain. The violence is actually being carried out behind the curtain and we can only see the frantic movement of the drapes. The camera slowly tracks forward and there appears a hand from behind the curtain, searching desperately for something until it finally finds a pair of scissors. The murder takes place off-screen. The camera after showing us the hand of Alice grasping the scissors retreats slowly from the site of action to a medium shot of the drapes again as if distancing itself from the act of murder. As the camera tracks back, we are greeted with another hand coming out of the curtain, but this hand is limp and lifeless.

[7] In the strangling scene of Miriam in *Strangers on a Train*, after a close shot of Miriam's face and the hands of Bruno menacingly coming toward her and gripping her neck, the camera cuts to an extreme close shot of Miriam's glasses that fall on the ground where the entire strangling is shown in a distorted, grotesque form with the jarring music of the carnival in the background. Again, we are twice removed from the site of actual violence on-screen. In *Blackmail* and *Strangers on a Train* visuals do not help us. Our vision is either deliberately obscured or is escorted away from the actual violence.

be used as shields by the audience. The torture is stark, brutal, and unabashed. Even after the invasion of the body, the camera does not spare us. The sudden attack upon the viewer of an extreme close shot of Brenda's dead face with her protruding eyes almost at the point of bursting accompanied by a jarring background score, which literally cause us to jump, is a testament to how far we can go to punish and tame and contain bodies that refuse to yield. This shot is followed by another medium-close shot of her face with her tongue sticking out. Earlier, while Rusk carries out the task of torturing her body, the camera carries out the task of dissecting her body through extreme close shots of different parts of her anatomy: her legs hanging out of the couch, her arm outstretched, her breast, her throat while the tie cuts at her skin, all giving us a distinct impression of dismemberment.

The ravaging and fragmentation of the body are carried out simultaneously. It took three days to complete this disturbing scene and a body double was used while showing parts of Brenda's anatomy—another instance of a body being replicated, readjusted, and realigned. The victim's bulging eyeballs, her legs sticking out of the couch, her arm reaching out, and her tongue jutting out of her mouth are all that "protrudes" from her body. They are stretched due to excruciating pain; they are "prolonged" as a final desperate attempt at self-preservation—a live body's efforts to prevent itself from becoming a "grotesque" specimen.

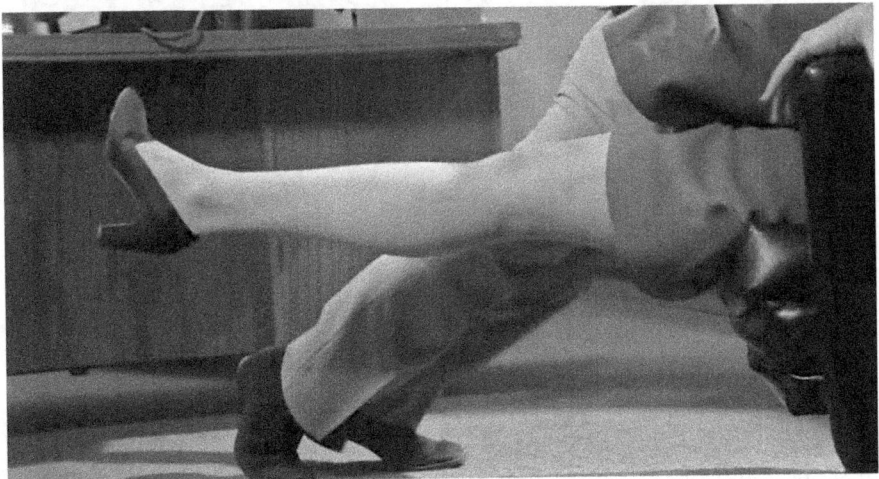

Figure 4.7 Brenda's stretched leg in the rape scene, *Frenzy*.

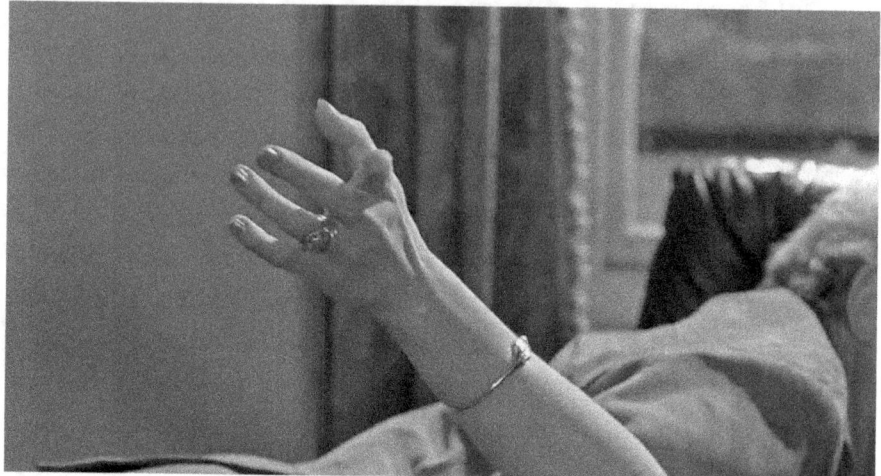

Figure 4.8 Brenda's hands reaching out in the rape scene, *Frenzy*.

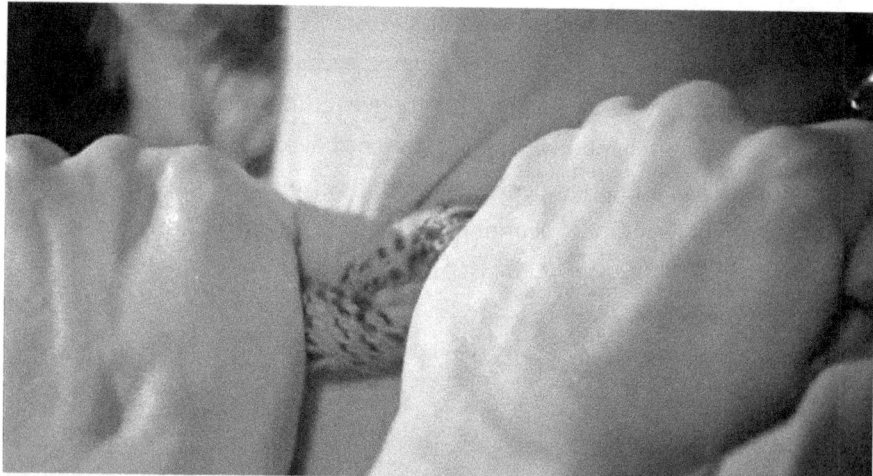

Figure 4.9 Strangling of Brenda, *Frenzy*.

Surveillance and Voyeurism

While contemporary slashers thrived on sex and gore, films on crime detection refrained from a blatant display of lurid torture. Voyeurism is a major concern in slashers and surveillance is a detective film's forte. Sex, gore, and excess are stuff voyeurs feed on. Surveillance, on the other hand, strives to monitor. It is wary of excess. Hitchcock, in *Frenzy*, combines crime detection with sex and torture. Hitchcock's films bring forth the disconcerting possibility that surveillance is usually a façade that conceals convenient voyeurism. Often in his films surveillance becomes blatantly voyeuristic (*Frenzy*), while voyeurism easily slips into surveillance (*Rear Window, Psycho*).

The dead Brenda, with every minute part of her reduced to images, at the mercy of crime investigators, photographers, forensic experts, the entire court, and the witnesses, traverses a long path of violation against which she has no defense. It is her body on trial as it becomes an object of fantasies, snide remarks at pubs, and irreverent analysis at dinner table conversations. Her past is dug out, judged, and sullied. Discussions and inquiries work to dehumanize the victim and objectify the body thereby controlling and eroticizing the entire process of investigation. Joy Palmer in "Tracing bodies: Gender, genre, and forensic detective fiction" (2001) draws upon Patricia Cornwell's novel *Postmortem* (1990) to show the innate sexism of this corrective gaze through a perplexing vigilance of the body:

> The novel begins with Scarpetta's journey to the home of a dead woman who has been brutally raped by a serial rapist. On the husband's request that her exposed body be covered up and hidden from the view of the numerous male police officers roaming the house—"I don't want every son of a bitch and his brother staring at her!"—Marino assures the husband that the gaze of those around her is nothing but respectful. So begins, according to Scarpetta, the "sweet balm of lies."
>
> (60)

Palmer further cites *From Potter's Field* (1995, the sixth novel of the series) and points out how Scarpetta, despite being a woman investigator, is unable to transcend "the ideological potency of the clinical, disciplinary gaze" and views the victim as a "territory to be discovered and marked, equating her body to 'geography', her belly a 'flat plain', her breasts 'gentle slopes'. It seems that Scarpetta perpetuates the sexual vision that characterizes medical looking relations" (Palmer 2001, 65). Surveillance ensures a fixed power relation as it is supposed to do. The roving examining gaze of the investigator invades the body, almost replicating the rapist. Ironically, the invasion does not require privacy.

Carried out in the name of an investigation, the prodding and surveying of the dead matter are a public affair, done mostly by men whose regulatory role would construct the body as an object to be derided and desired at the same time.

Hitchcock's *Frenzy*, similarly, betrays a direct link between the physical brutality meted out to women and the rampant institutional misogyny within the legal system. In the case of a crime novel, the physical features of the deceased are carefully mapped—the complexion, weight, height, composition, and marks on the body are stated clearly. In films dealing with murder, especially a film such as *Frenzy*, where the viewer becomes a voluntary or an involuntary participant in both the rape and the murder, and is also given the privileged position of seeing the dead body at close quarters with the camera offering close shots of the female victim, the body is discovered in minute portions. Each portion is then analyzed from a clinical gaze, but such seeing usually functions effectively to inscribe social identity into the body. The individuality and cultural location of the once-alive body are reconstructed through material signs on the skin that is gauged by a pronounced gendered prodding. Unsurprisingly the clinical or the investigative gaze eroticizes the body of the victim. By being passive and helpless, the corpse partakes in the conventional/expected traits of a docile "feminized" body.

Scrutinizing an immobile inanimate female body by the empiricist rationalist gaze of a male investigator is one of the markers of the genre that has been fiercely patriarchal from its very inception. Surveillance here is used as a tool to rub that domination in. In *Frenzy* Brenda is a divorced independent woman who runs a successful business; Babs is seen as the other woman in Blaney's life, a confident working woman, one who does not have qualms about spending nights with a man charged with murder. All these add to the way their bodies are viewed. The feisty women who could hold up their own are reduced to ridiculous specimens to be searched, scrutinized, and dismissed: from the criminal's perspective they are bodies that have served their purpose and, therefore, bodies that no longer matter; from the perspective of the law they are bodies that are reduced to matter and therefore can still serve a purpose, that is, to track a criminal, and for the bystanders, they are bodies to be used as the stuff of gruesome fantasy to be sexually constructed and castigated again.

Hitchcock and Feminist Theory: Misogyny or Ambivalence?

Although Raymond Durgnat in *A Long Hard Look at Psycho* (2002) suggests that the art of observing can never be reduced only to sexual gratification or merely to a voyeuristic or scopophiliac predisposition, we cannot ignore the long list of psychoanalytic feminist critics who speak of Hitchcock's misogyny, or at best, ambivalent portrayal of his women characters. Films like *Blackmail* (1929), *Rebecca* (1940), *Dial M for Murder* (1954), *Notorious* (1946), *Strangers on a Train* (1951), *Vertigo* (1958), *Psycho* (1960), *The Birds* (1963), *Marnie* (1964), and finally *Frenzy* (1972) are heavily steeped in violence and brutality aimed at women that more than suggest a connection between the filmmaker (Hitchcock) and mainstream cinema's deep-rooted patriarchal predisposition.

Perhaps Alfred Hitchcock can neither be labeled as utterly misogynistic nor is he largely sympathetic to women and their plight in patriarchy. His work is characterized by a thoroughgoing ambivalence about femininity. As Sidney Gottlieb, speaking of Hitchcock's "Nova Grows Up" in *Hitchcock on Hitchcock* (vol.1), points out:

> we should ... not miss the clear signs that the prospect of a young woman growing up in front of him both charms and disturbs Hitchcock. Barely beneath the surface, we see what may well be a characteristic mixture of adoration, desire, jealousy (fantasizing about the 'tragedy' of getting her 'into the hands of Hollywood makeup men'), manipulation, and active hostility.
> (1995, 71)

It cannot be denied that his films like *Blackmail*, *Psycho*, and *Strangers on a Train* suffer from the infection of misogyny, but it is equally true that he also has the most impressive gallery of extremely strong, perceptive, and sharp women characters in his films: Alice White (Anny Ondra) in *Blackmail*, the absent yet potently present Rebecca de Winter in *Rebecca*, Charlie Newton (Teresa Wright) in *Shadow of a Doubt*, Alicia Huberman (Ingrid Bergman) in *Notorious*, Miriam Haines (Laura Elliott) in *Strangers on a Train*, Margot Wendice (Grace Kelly) in *Dial M for Murder*, Lisa Fremont (Grace Kelly) in *Rear Window*, Josephine McKenna (Doris Day) in *The Man Who Knew Too*

Much, Judy Barton (Kim Novak) in *Vertigo*, Marion Crane (Janet Leigh) in *Psycho*, Melanie Daniels (Tippi Hedren) in *The Birds*, Marnie Edgar (Tippi Hedren) in *Marnie*—all undoubtedly occupy a very significant space in Hitchcock's filmography.

So, the question remains—why this ambivalence? Feminist theory took up a distinct stance on the objectification, exclusion, and silence of women in cinematic narratives. By recognizing and exploring the centrality of the power of the gaze, Laura Mulvey's essay "Visual Pleasure and Narrative Cinema" (1975), the founding document of feminist film criticism, takes Hitchcock's films as examples to show how in classic Hollywood cinema, the active possessing and devouring gaze is implicitly male, and how women are reduced to passive objects of male voyeuristic pleasure. Women exist simply to cater to the desires and express the anxieties of the male spectator, and by implication, women spectators can only have a masochistic relation to the cinema. However, understanding the limitations of assuming sexual difference based strictly on binary oppositions (masculinity-active, femininity-passive), Mulvey published another article in 1981, "Afterthoughts on Visual Pleasure and Narrative Cinema" which took "transvestism" into account and attempted to analyze a woman's oscillation between a male-coded and a female-coded mode of viewing (24–35). This brings us to another important aspect that informs female spectatorship—the idea of female bisexuality. By taking female bisexuality as a reference point, will we then be able to analyze Hitchcock's and Hollywood's treatment of women in a better light?

Gertrude Koch while addressing the question of "why women go to men's movies" focuses on Freud's theory of female bisexuality which is based on women's pre-oedipal attachment to her mother. The idea of this attachment opened up new avenues for Freud and led him to revise his theories of childhood sexuality as he recognized the fundamental asymmetry in male and female development (1985, 110). Tania Modleski, citing the example of Koch, states, "The female's attachment to the mother often goes 'unresolved' throughout her life and coexists with her later heterosexual relationships" (2005, 6). In her article on *Rebecca,* Modleski attempts a "female oedipal trajectory." She argues that some of Hitchcock's films "do allow for the limited expression of a specifically female desire" (Modleski 1982, 2). Teresa de

Lauretis in *Alice Doesn't* (1984), quite in line with Modleski, takes Hitchcock's *Rebecca* and *Vertigo* to explore the workings of female spectatorship. Teresa de Lauretis argues that female spectatorship is a far more complex issue that cannot simply be assessed through the lens of masochism or a simple male-active/female-passive binary. She speaks of the dilemma inherent in female spectatorship as a woman viewer is trapped in a "double desire." She becomes a site of merger between a passive (usually female) object and an active (usually male) subject identifying with both at once.

Although in *Psycho*, the mother/son relationship constitutes the core of the film, the reference to Marion's mother by Sam in the opening scene of the film strikes a discordant note in an otherwise cozy exchange between two lovers. A number of Hitchcock films revolve around the pivot of a mother/daughter relationship, which, at times, constitutes the main conflict of the films. In *To Catch a Thief*, Frances Stevens (Grace Kelly) is the daughter of Jessie Stevens (Jessie Royce Landis) who has such a forbearing personality that Frances has to struggle hard not to lose her individuality. Again, *Rebecca* is all about a woman's problems of over-identification with another woman. Marnie's problem, as far as patriarchy is concerned, is an excessive attachment to her mother that prevents her from achieving a "properly feminine" sexual relationship with a man. Man's need to prohibit, suppress, and punish female voyeurism is thus attributable to their concern about women's pleasure in looking at other women as women's bisexuality could make them "competitors for the male preserve" (Modleski 2005, 6). Modleski further elaborates that masculine identity is bound up with feminine identity on the individual psychological plane as well as at the level of society. Female bisexuality is an uneasy reminder of male bisexuality which problematizes patriarchal domination (2005, 8). We may add here that woman's bisexuality further threatens the patriarchal order in two different ways, the first by making women absent-minded or oblivious to the order, and the second by assaulting the active-passive binary.

If the construct of power on the gender axis rests on the Masculine (active)–Feminine (passive) binary both on-screen and in the audience then the corresponding voyeuristic binary would be male voyeurism and masochistic voyeurism. But bisexuality destabilizes this patriarchal binary by problematizing gender relations at two levels:

Level-I: Same-sex relation—the male is stripped of his masculinity. By implication, the female no longer needs to be feminine. Thus "Masculine-Feminine" binary is lost to patriarchy.

This Level-I crisis of patriarchy is dealt with in two ways:

i. by suppressing same-sex relations overtly; and
ii. by subverting same-sex relations: to make the "masculine-feminine" binary sneak into it.

Level-II: Heterosexual relation of a bisexual—the subversion of same-sex relation, that is, the sneaking of the "masculine-feminine" binary mentioned above (ii) breaks down. The masculine in female-female relation needs to be feminine now. The feminine in male-male relation has to be masculine now.

The entire structure of gender power based on the active-passive binary is, therefore, being interrogated and problematized at more than one level and the violence toward women in classic Hollywood cinema may well be traced to these basic anxieties of men to maintain the safe divide between the dominant and the dominated. It is a Norman Bates who is a victim of such a strict divide. He becomes a degendered, traumatized human repository of a guilt-ridden, anxiety-ridden society of men limited by their self-prescribed role of the dominant, burdened by their sense of power. Norman, in the end, is a character liberated from the limitation of gender and its corresponding problematic nature of strict classification. Yet we feel a kind of pain and fear for Norman as we witness his transformation. We tend to wonder as the film ends—is "it" Norman Bates or is "it" his mother? Is the pathetic creature before us a "feminized" male or a "masculinized" female?

5

Fellow-Stuffers: Post-*Psycho* Body Horrors

"It rubs the lotion on its skin": *The Silence of the Lambs, Perfume*, and Body Horror

Jane Eastoe in her book *The Art of Taxidermy* (2012) speaks of the role of skin in taxidermy: "Skin is valuable; it is eaten, worn, upholstered and fetishistic. It is the raw material of taxidermy" (Loc. 95 of 1132). This "raw material" and its "value" that Eastoe speaks of have been exploited by Body Horrors for decades. Body Horrors from the literary text of Mary Shelley's *Frankenstein* (1818) to the cinematic texts of *Psycho* (1960), *The Silence of the Lambs* (Demme 1991), *Perfume: The Story of a Murderer* (Tykwer 2006), *The Skin I Live In* (Almodovar 2011), and many others use human skin in every way as described by Eastoe: it is ingested, worn, upholstered, and fetishized. Alfred Hitchcock's *Psycho* and *Frenzy* act as significant predecessors of films such as *The Silence of the Lambs* and *Perfume* where the dead point to a lack in the live bodies that require violence to fulfill themselves. They reveal that fear, vulnerability, and weakness reside in the very power that is displayed by the "machismo" of the killers.

Judith Halberstam in *Skin Shows: Gothic Horror and the Technology of Monsters* (1995) attempts to understand both these exploiting and exploited bodies that have shaped the course of the history of Body Horrors in cinema. Halberstam begins her book with a description of Buffalo Bill in Jonathan Demme's *The Silence of the Lambs* donning his "woman suit" (one that he creates by killing and flaying women) and prancing before the mirror:

> Sitting in his basement sewing hides, Buffalo Bill makes his monster a sutured beast, a patchwork of gender, sex, and sexuality. Skin, in this morbid scene, represents the monstrosity of surfaces and as Buffalo Bill dresses up in his suit and prances in front of the mirror, he becomes a layered body.
>
> (1995, 1)

Buffalo Bill is used by Halberstam as an instance to show the path traveled by monsters from nineteenth-century texts of horror to contemporary texts of vulnerable human bodies. According to Halberstam, while the nineteenth-century Gothic monsters represent myriad binaries by becoming bodies that shelter the external and the internal, the male and the female, the animal and the human, the familiar and the unfamiliar, the proletarian and the elite, postmodern representations of monstrosity have become skin deep: "The immediate visibility of a Buffalo Bill, the way in which he makes the surface itself monstrous transforms the cavernous monstrosity of Jekyll/Hyde, Dorian Gray, or Dracula into a beast who is all body and no soul" (1995, 1).

Creating a body without a soul is a sure way to represent a social misfit. The body of Buffalo Bill (Ted Levine) in *The Silence of the Lambs* and the body of Jean Baptiste Grenouille (Ben Whishaw) in *Perfume: The Story of a Murderer* are socially stigmatized. Buffalo Bill is denied a sex-change operation several times. His sewing and donning of a layer of flayed female skin is his way of gaining individual agency as a reaction against socially imposed restrictions. The state-imposed prescriptions that deny him his personhood ironically lead him to capture unsuspecting women and brutally take away their personhood and their very lives from them. He forces his victims to rub a lotion over their skin that would loosen the skin so that he could strip it off easily after their death. The pace of the loosening of the skin determines the number of days the victim would survive. When the skin is loose enough to be taken off, the victim is murdered. The slackening of the victim's skin is akin to her moving toward an asexual body. As the skin sags, it loses its "female" contours, blurring the sexual identity of the victim. Then this skin gets transferred from the female body to the male one, symbolically also transferring its sexuality.

The skin works as a site of gendered norms by which Buffalo Bill performs. The skin that he dons and the vagina that he creates for himself encourage him to "prance" in front of his mirror and perform like a socially prescribed "female" body. The performance however has to be confined to his basement. Even in the privacy of his basement, his body ironically follows social dictates. His recreated "female self" moves in front of the mirror adhering to the rules of a female "socialized body." Buffalo Bill flouts societal norms by assigning himself a skin that society has refused him, but he conforms to the gendered role that a "female" body should abide by. The easy-to-be-flayed loose skin, on the other hand, petrifies the victim and becomes a chief ingredient of this Body Horror. After all, skin turning against its body is a recurrent feature of Body Horrors. Halberstam's discussion on the function of the skin in literary and filmic Body Horrors in *Skin Shows* is relevant in the context of remade bodies as it helps us to detect an analogy between the texts of Body Horror and the art of taxidermy.

The victims in Tom Tykwer's *Perfume: The Story of a Murderer*, on the other hand, are killed for their scent. Scent is an inherent part of the skin. The extreme close shots of the skimming of wax from the smooth skin and hair of dead women litter the entire setting of Tykwer's *Perfume*. The bodies, surprisingly, without being flayed, have the look of flayed ones deprived as they are of hair and scent. The bodies seem shorn of their epidermis as if scent forms an unseen layer of the skin. The skin is left raw, shaved, and exposed in the middle of the streets of Grasse. This invisible layer is what Grenouille craves. Jean-Baptiste Grenouille in *Perfume* has a skin that lacks the only thing that he covets the most—scent. His body is odorless and his only obsession is odor. He creates a perfume by scraping and extracting the scent of murdered women's skin and hair, a scent that has the power to enslave the entire world. Shaved, naked female bodies provide fluids for his coveted perfume. Toward the end, he pours the perfume on his body, and the people around him, unable to resist the lure of the scent, tear him to pieces. The scent that he sought throughout his life pervades his body and liberates him from his loveless forlorn world.

Halberstam, speaking of nineteenth-century monsters, states: "Skin (in nineteenth-century monsters) becomes a kind of metonym for the human; and its color, its pallor, its shape mean everything within a semiotic of monstrosity" (1995, 7). While describing this "monstrous skin" she takes both literary texts of the nineteenth century and the films of the twentieth century into consideration: "Skin might be too tight (Frankenstein's creature), too dark (Hyde), too pale (Dracula), too superficial (Dorian Gray's canvas), too loose (Leatherface), or too sexed (Buffalo Bill)" (1995, 7). In this catalog of the skin of the misfits, the name of Norman Bates is missing. The first film which blatantly brings out the chilling aspects of skin as a raw material way before *The Texas Chainsaw Massacre*, *The Silence of the Lambs*, or *Perfume* is *Psycho*. Hitchcock's film *Psycho* brought and situated the idea of a borrowed skin firmly within mainstream cinema. Norman Bates' hobby, taxidermy (an art that deals with hollow structures and skins that were once alive), is a perfect art for a man with a hollow life, a life that he seeks to stuff with the dead skin of his mother. *Psycho* not only speaks of the monstrous skin, but it also speaks of the vulnerable skin, that is helpless to defend itself from being sliced, spliced, and spiced. Skin in *Psycho* (in the cases of both Norman and Norma) is too human, too alive.

"The Things a Madman's Love Can Do ... ": *Psycho*, *The Skin I Live In*, and Surgical Art Horror

From humanities and social sciences to physiology and cosmetology, most disciplines have charted their ever-evolving theoretical concerns on human skin. Skin has been a crucial factor in determining identity and difference. Scarification, piercing, tattoos, masks, cosmetic surgeries, and various other inscriptions on the skin have long been looked upon as pointers of race, gender, sexuality, ethnicity, and as bearers of political and cultural status, and of the sacred and the profane. Since the 1990s, greater emphasis has been placed on the materiality of skin and its subjectivity while considering the body as a cultural construct. Scholars like Pippa Brush in *Metaphors of Inscription* (1998), Bryan S. Turner in *The Body and Society* (2008), and Atkinson and Young in *Flesh Journeys* (2001), among others, focus on the cultural and material reading of reforged skin and react against a "disembodied" representation of body and skin. Speaking on cosmetic surgery, Brush asserts that we cannot ignore

> the materiality of the body and the social contexts within which bodies are experienced and constructed. While the rhetoric surrounding cosmetic surgery denies the physical process ... so theories of the body which stress the body's plasticity also deny the materiality of that process and the cultural and social contexts within which the body is always placed.
>
> (1998, 22)

Remade bodies, and the preservation of those remade bodies, by rearranging the skin that clothes them form a major point of connection between the art of cosmetology and the art of taxidermy. One has a living body as its canvas, and the other a dead one.

The three strands of destruction, recreation, and preservation of a customized body are brought forth in the anatomical reconstruction of a male body into a female one in Pedro Almodóvar's *The Skin I Live In* (2011). The story of an obsessed scientist, Robert Ledgard (Antonio Banderas), who transforms Vicente (Jan Cornet), who he thinks has raped his daughter, into a spitting image of his dead wife, Gal (who was burnt in a car crash and whom he almost nursed back to life but ultimately failed as she committed suicide after seeing her face without a skin) speaks of skin as a trap. Robert Ledgard takes a male body, emasculates it, and then assigns it a vagina, breasts, a "perfect" body, and a face that he is obsessed with—the face and body of a woman whom he could not properly tame, a woman who ran away with his half-brother, Zeca (Roberto Alamo). When Robert discovers that another man (Vicente) has apparently molested his daughter (Norma, played by Blanca Suarez), he conveniently finds in him an object on which he could heap all his anger, all his frustrations, and transform him into a "toy" that would pay for all his past failures—thus Vicente becomes Vera (Elena Anaya). Filmmakers who belong to the 1950s and 1960s noir and, later, the 1980s and 1990s slasher genres, are known to transform fiery wild femme fatales into domesticated objects. Almodóvar, on the other hand, in a marked departure from his predecessors, chooses to problematize the very codes of sex and gender. He creates confusion in the very realm of representation by transforming a man into a woman.

Sexually fluid body is one of the favorite premises of Almodóvar on which he builds his oeuvre. *Labyrinths of Passion* (1982), *Dark Habits* (1983), *Law of Desire* (1987), *All About My Mother* (1999), *Talk to Her* (2002), and *Bad Education* (2004) all speak of bodies that are extremely volatile in terms of both sexual identity and sexual orientation. Clothes that form an important marker of a body's identity are also meticulously plotted and designed in his films in keeping with the protean bodies that crowd his films.

The imagery of clothes runs throughout *The Skin I Live In*: they are bought, sold, resold, exhibited, torn apart, stitched, and used as raw materials for artwork. Clothing is the most basic form of deception as it hides who we are and also, by functioning as a tool of "repeated stylization of the body" molds the body "within a highly rigid regulatory frame" (Butler 2012, 45). Kaja Silverman argues: "Dress is one of the most important cultural implements for articulating and territorializing human corporeality—for mapping its erotogenic zones and for affixing a sexual identity" (Silverman 1996, 83). *The Skin I Live In* usually shows Vera either naked or wearing her "second skin" to "mold" and "protect" a body created by her twenty-first-century Frankenstein. The skin-dress is smooth, seamless and surprisingly asexual. Although it acts as a surrogate of human skin, it brings forth a body where the breasts are without nipples and the genitalia are absent. It is a body in the making, or a body that remains unfinished. The skin-dress is a metaphoric rendition of Vicente's sexual identity gradually undergoing metamorphosis as he is forced to abandon one skin and put on another.

Vicente/Vera's body is a living stage where momentary sexual identities are violently played out. The core identity that Vicente desperately tries to cling to clashes with the body assigned to him. Like Louise Bourgeois' patched-up sculptures shown in the film, Vicente's body is also patched up with snippets of artificially constructed female anatomy methodically etched on his male body thereby negating the very notion of sexual fixity. Vera/Vicente's body is a performance of contradictions where we find a simultaneous birth and death of gender construction and a repeated surfacing, smudging, and resurfacing of sexual identities that oscillate between how Vera appears and who Vicente is. Clothes happen to be a significant marker of that vacillation. It acts as a veil to conceal the rebellion seething within and it also acts as a material of compulsory incarceration. There is an unmistakable dramatic quality in Vera's clothes that include her skin suit. The uncanniness of Vera's skin suit arises from its close resemblance to a recognizable female body and its simultaneous absence. Clothes function as masks that both protect one's privacy and yet aid one to communicate with others. They act as shields, as forms to cloister oneself from others. They concurrently help one to hide behind intended identities (Spooner 2004, 124–5).

Vera's skin suit in the film performs as a mask. But the mask is contradictory to the identity of the wearer. The clothes alienate the body that it covers. Rather than protecting Vera's privacy, it makes Vera's body surface-centric where the exterior, constructed by Robert Ledgard, does not conceal but rather exposes. It does not aid in communication, but rather alienates Vera from her surroundings. Vera's mask has three layers—the transgenic skin plastered on her by Ledgard, the skin suit that molds that artificial skin, and the clothes that hide the skin suit. This three-layered mask projects Vera as a constant exhibit where there is neither concealment nor communication. Her clothes do not lend her an intended identity, but rather an absence of identity. The biological features imposed on her by her maker, despite being flawless, bring forth her featurelessness, her void. It is, as if, through the construction of this body on the female/male threshold, Almodovar, blatantly exhibits the fear of what Tania Modleski infers in *The Women Who Knew Too Much* (2005)—an uneasy reminder of male bisexuality with all its attendant anxieties and crises.

The Trapped Body

Norman, in one of the most moving moments of *Psycho*, says, "I think that we're all in our private traps, clamped in them, and none of us can ever get out. We scratch and claw, but only at the air, only at each other. And for all of it, we never budge an inch." *Psycho* has a wide range of stuffed birds—owls, crows, pheasants, and songbirds. It is their once-lived skin that are shaped in different postures in Norman's parlor. The birds are as much trapped in their skin as the humans metaphorically are. The skin and the skeleton of Norma Bates are what both Norma and Norman cannot escape. In *The Skin I Live In*, Vicente's post-surgery female body is both a material and a psychological trial of his subjectivity. It is the systematic, forced reconceptualization and reconstruction of a body through transgenesis, vaginoplasty, created layers of artificial skin and a well-fitted skin suit through which a sense of claustrophobia and incarceration is created in the film.

Like Norma Bates, Vicente/Vera's space of confinement does not limit itself to his/her room but shrinks further to the confines of his/her body. The film opens with the outside view of El Cigarral and as the camera pans from the Villa board to the gate and into the room of Vera, we get four consecutive shots that suggest a gradual narrowing down of space: a close shot of the iron bars of the main gate, followed by another close shot of the wired mesh behind window bars with a blurred image of Vera within, succeeded by an extreme close shot of a camera looking at Vera in her room, and finally a medium close shot of her body tightly fitted in her skin-apparel. These four establishing shots of the film introduce the idea of restriction through surveillance and confinement, through literal and metaphoric images of a prison coming closer and closer until it invades the very body of the protagonist, from iron gates to wired mesh, to window bars, to cameras, and finally to a body-hugging suit that acts as a surrogate skin, controlling and shaping the body within.

For Vera, the inevitability of confinement comes in the form of a membrane that covers her. The created skin pasted on her body is a tough derma that provides no scope of permeability. It is a skin that is impervious to insect bites and flames. This thick coat of protection serves as armor. But armors also suggest restricted movement. They are heavy, unyielding, and claustrophobic. The skin as a prison is a recurrent motif of the film that finds a concrete visual representation in the scene where we are offered a close shot of Vera's naked

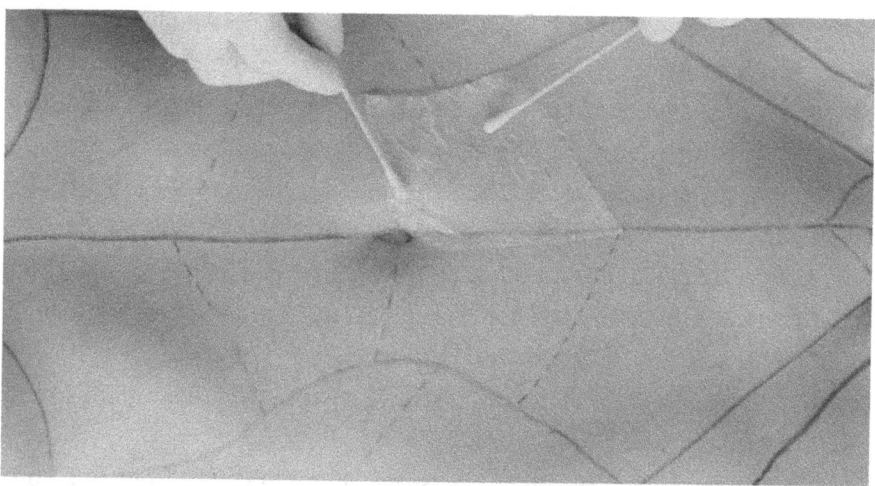

Figure 5.1 Vera's body being marked and mapped by Robert Ledgard, *The Skin I Live In*.

body on the operating table. We detect clear lines on the skin of Vera that demarcate the throat from the face, the legs and arms from the torso, and the breasts from the abdomen. The lines thus drawn seem a visual equivalent to prison bars. It seems we are viewing the body of Vera through the prism of incarcerating lines that ironically join and separate her. This is followed by a bird's eye view shot of a prostrate Vera, static and immobile, arrested by lines that neatly tie and yet separate her anatomy and her body appears as one that is carting its prison with it.

[M]y Ungainly Body Stumping over the Mud Flats with a Look of Transformation[1]

Robert Ledgard in Pedro Almodovar's *The Skin I Live In* parallels Norman Bates in *Psycho* as he seeks to fill his empty life with created dead skin mortared on a live body. Unlike a taxidermist who rearranges a corpse skin, Robert Ledgard "recreates" an already existent live "derma" by fusing it with an artificially constructed one. *The Skin I Live In* is a surgical horror that can also be seen as a Frankenstein's fantasy that predictably turns against him. Vera in *The Skin I Live In* is the creation of a man, a body born out of the labors of an obsessed surgeon. Here the biological material (Vicente/Vera's body) itself becomes a narrative of transmutations that feeds on desire, obsession, destruction, and reconstruction. Anatomically a complete opposite of Frankenstein's Creature, Vicente/Vera's body is etched with the history of conversion, suppression, and the eternal quest for an ephemeral object. Skin is shown in myriad ways in the film: marked, dissected, spliced open, stitched together, peeled off, or covered with layers of stockings, bandages, and masks. Like the narrative of the film (with its frequent use of the flashback) that slowly unfolds before the viewers, the sheets of Vicente's skin are peeled off layer after layer until we get to the raw skin of a "created"

---

[1] Carson, "The Glass Essay."

Vera. Like the imagery of clothes that runs throughout the film, skin is also used by Almodóvar as a raiment that encapsulates both identity and deception, vulnerability and resistance.

Vera's skin is not her own. It is a product of transgenesis, a mixture of animal and human blood. By being immune to external threats, burns, or insect bites, the skin is dead. So, in Vera's body, the biological narrative that taxidermy relates is reversed. Here a live body is dressed with a skin that is not real, a skin that has not been "lived." Robert keeps the body alive but changes the skin, making it tougher, desensitized, and immune to the ravages of time. Unlike a taxidermist, who "arranges the skin," Robert Ledgard replaces the old skin with a new one that he artificially creates in his laboratory. The anatomical death of Vicente, therefore, leads to the birth of Vera.

Both Robert in *The Skin I Live In* and Norman in *Psycho* strive to make their recreated skin look alive. Norman's longing to see his mother alive is so acute that he becomes his mother at times. It is only through the parched dead skin of his mother that Norman lives. Robert, on the other hand, creates a whole new customized body that he can command and control. He thrives only through the perfect, unblemished, artificial skin of a forcedly created lover. "Live" skin flayed from dead bodies, and "dead" skin coated over live bodies supposedly complete these "monsters." This sense of completion and accomplishment, paradoxically, liberates and cages these obsessed creators.

Both *Psycho* and *The Skin I Live In* speak of the skin that reflects their creator's monstrosity. They focus on bodies that are helpless to defend themselves from the very materials that give them unfamiliar shapes. Consequently, both Norma Bates and Vera Cruz (though anatomical opposites) turn out to be grotesque trophies of their creators. Their bodies become wish-fulfilling spaces where the past can be visited and altered at will. In *The Skin I Live In* the monster does this by creating a liminal sexual identity out of his victim. In *Psycho*, the wish-fulfilling is more complex, where the monster not only transforms the victim into an unfamiliar shape but also transforms himself into a state of sexual liminality to take on, at times, the role of the victim.

What problematizes the monster-victim discourse is the blurring of the monster-victim dichotomy itself. Monsters like Norman Bates, Buffalo Bill, and Jean-Baptiste Grenouille, are themselves victims of social marginalization. It is usually a "lack" that the "monsters"/"victims" try to fill. Buffalo Bill's failed attempt to become a transgender person (because he is not "not-man-enough" to meet the requisites of the sex-change operation) leads him to create his own hide by stitching the skin of murdered women to get himself a body he craves for. His penis is a "lack" that he hides behind his created vagina as he poses before the mirror in his basement to fulfill his desire for a coveted anatomy. For Jean-Baptiste Grenouille the "lack" is the absence of scent in his body, for Norman Bates, the "lack" is the would-be absence of his mother. Robert Ledgard too is a lonely soul tormented by personal failures, a recluse living in a villa cut off from the stream of life outside.

"Mind If I Cut In?": Pleasure, Power, and the Mad Surgeon

The post-1990s world of body modification, cosmetology, and Hagen's Body Worlds[2] have given birth to the contemporary clinical culture of which Almodóvar's *The Skin I Live In* is an example. Nonconsensual plastic surgery in the film reminds us of all the mad scientists and doctors like Dr. Moreau and Dr. Heiter that populate surgical horrors from H. G. Wells' *The Island of Dr. Moreau* (1896) to Tom Six's *The Human Centipede* (2009), with their obsession of anatomical mutation of humans/beasts. They bring forth the ultimate reduction of humans/beasts to their basic anatomical and scatological terrain. The dread of this surgical art horror film stems from a complete disregard of the victim as an individual. Robert's Vera (much in the vein of Scottie's Madeleine in *Vertigo*) is a work of art, an imitation of a body he could not control. And the fact that he had to transform a male body

---

[2] Gunther von Hagen's "Body Worlds" are a series of corporeal exhibitions of human and nonhuman plastinated skinned corpses that are extremely popular. It adds the twin motifs of science and spectacle, education and entertainment to our contemporary world of exhibitionary culture.

into a female one to inflict the lowest forms of humiliation on it goes to show that mere violence and pain are not enough, the body has to acknowledge its subjection by accepting its position in the age-old gender hierarchy that the mainstream prescribes. As Mulvey-Roberts (2018) in *Dangerous Bodies* states, "The most sinister reason for carrying out sexual surgery on men and women is to control sexuality" (2018, 92). Mulvey-Roberts reads Bram Stoker's *Dracula* (1897) as a text where vampirism is a "trope for an invented female pathology" where Stoker prescribes "surgical solutions" (2018, 93) for aberrant sexual behavior. While Mulvey-Roberts speaks primarily of female castration in her reading of *Dracula*, Almodóvar in *The Skin I Live In* explores the crisis of self-identity, masculinity, and femininity by bestowing "perfect" breasts and genitalia on a male body.

Psycho, *The Silence of the Lambs*, *Perfume*, and *The Skin I Live In* bring forth the disturbing possibility that medical practices, like body modifications and plastic surgeries, which are usually seen as voluntary choices of individuals, may also be used to deny personhood. When consent is absent (much in the vein of taxidermy), cosmetic surgery, even if it culls out a beautiful body, is no less a punitive measure than scarification, tattoos, and brands inscribed on bodies by authoritarian regimes. Cosmetic surgery can also be read as a form of bodily inscription. As Brush suggests, if "the body is—metaphorically—a site of inscription to various degrees for various theorists, then cosmetic surgery can be seen, at one level, as an example of the literal and explicit enactment of this process of inscription" (24). Cosmetic surgery can therefore be made a part of the structures of control. Vera's body is an example where such punitive inscriptions are etched. Like flaying, stitching, stuffing, and dismembering of the victims, surgeries too ensure not only a symbolic but a material yielding of personhood.

Skin-Art Merge: The Performers and the Protesters

Vera's body is reduced to a salvaged object (the body of Ledgard's dead wife, Gal) that can be preserved in Ledgard's menagerie. The volatile and fast-changing treatment of female anatomy on screen may find its parallel in a series of artwork that embellish the walls of El Cigarral. The nude Venus in the Titian paintings "Venus of Urbino" (1534) and "Venus with an Organist and Cupid" (1555) that fill the vast corridor of El Cigarral are testaments of bodies well-created, touched by eroticism, replete with an artist's thorough knowledge of human anatomy. The paintings are significantly placed in the passage that leads to Vera's room. The paintings serve as an index of what to expect once one opens the door of Vera's cell: a body created by a genius—perfect, beautiful, but untamed. The paintings in Robert's room and study include Henri Rousseau's "Eve" (amidst a mysterious dark jungle in "The Snake Charmer," 1907), and Guillermo Perez Villalta's Ariadne (a face without features, a face deprived of its sensory organs in "Dionysus Finds Ariadne in Naxos," 2008). Both these portraits highlight the obliteration of physical features. While Venus attracts us with her detailed anatomical beauty and symmetry, Ariadne attracts us with her complete absence of facial features, and Eve with her sinister eyes fascinates the viewer with an unknown dread. These three women may be read as the three stages of Vera's transformation. While Venus is what she appears to be, a perfect blend of beauty and eroticism, designed and choreographed with a perfect recipe by a meticulous maker, Ariadne (the mythical figure abandoned by one man and about to be accepted by another) is Vera in transition. Her masked face, her shaved head, and her body tightly fitted in stockings and bandages are the visual equivalent to Villalta's Ariadne, and finally, the dark Eve, the charmer Eve, the Eve whose sexuality is obscured by the darkness of the surrounding jungle is what Vera becomes, a menace who destroys her Frankenstein and, unlike his "Creature," triumphs.

Throughout the film, Vera is keen on destroying the art that she has come to represent. She engages in a tireless battle against this recurrent biological censorship and biological reforging by engaging her body's subversive powers to weave a counter-narrative in line with contemporary radical feminist artists who use their anatomy as a space of protest. The over-head close shots of Vera's torso—one with Ledgard's carefully drawn lines, and the other with blood streaks caused by self-mutilation—show how the very skin that has been branded with marks of proprietorship can be converted into a membrane of protest.

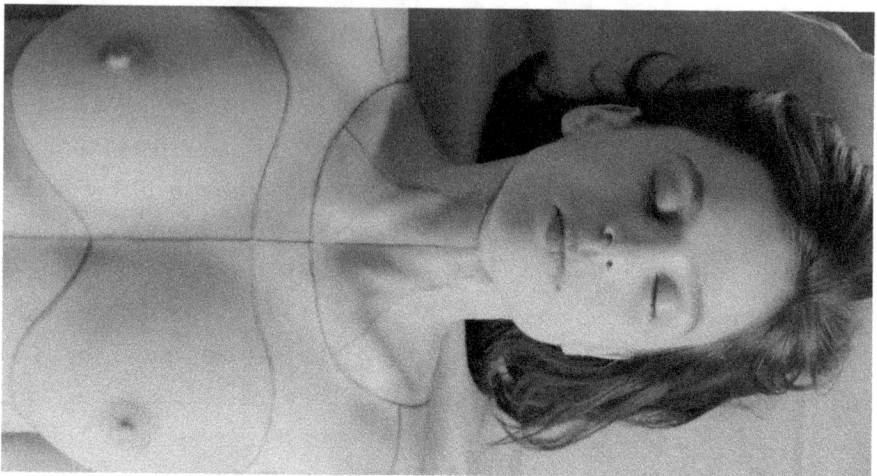

Figure 5.2 Vera's body with lines carved by Robert, *The Skin I Live In*.

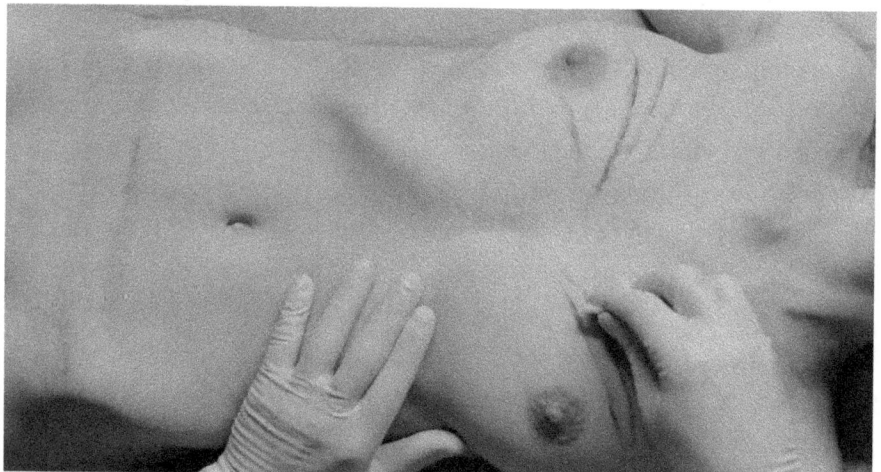

Figure 5.3 Vera's attempt at reclaiming her body, *The Skin I Live In*.

With self-inflicted cuts and bruises, Vera tries to break free from the metaphoric prison bars etched previously on her skin. She only has recourse to her own blood and ironically her own skin to obliterate the incarcerating lines of objectification and ownership of her creator. Her attempts at self-mutilation and her creation of patched-up plasticine sculptures inspired by the works of Louise Bourgeois, align her with radical performance artists like Marina

Abramovic,[3] Gina Pane, Ketty La Rocca, Suzanne Santoro, Silvia Giambrone,[4] and ORLAN[5] in a shared struggle to reclaim representation of their bodies usurped by male creators. It is this zone of vulnerability that becomes the zone of resistance, rebellion, and strength. Vera's act of inflicting pain on her body may be compared to the female artists' practice of using their own bodies as canvases. Pain, violence, and claustrophobia are often depicted through their violated and violating bodies. To challenge and interrogate the conventional representation of female bodies, female artists refrain from depicting the female body in a "positive" way. The bodies are tortured and mutilated to unveil the reality of such bodies in a patriarchal structure.

Skin, therefore, has the capability of subverting the marks of ownership imposed on it by an authoritarian force. Vera's initial scarring of her remade body (her breasts and her belly) and her slitting of her throat are gradually replaced by her strategic use of skin and clothes. The skin that alienates her from her previous body is used as a weapon against her maker. We see Vera in close shots when she meditates or exercises. Her immaculate skin is shown

---

[3] In 1974, Marina Abramovic staged a six-hour performance titled *Rhythm 0*, from 8 pm to 2 am, in a studio at Naples where she offered her body up as a canvas on which the spectators were allowed to confer their inscriptions with the aid of seventy-two objects kept on a table by her side. The objects included a rose, red paint, wine, lipstick, grapes, a whip, honey, a saw, a scalpel, a gun, and a bullet among other items. Abramovic in a signed document assured the audience that they could do anything on or to her body and they will not be held responsible for their actions. Her body would remain completely passive during the entire performance. The spectators who were now an active participant in the performance initially were timid, apprehensive, and controlled. With the passage of time, they grew more and more aggressive and the intensity of the invasion escalated as they pricked her skin with rose-stem, stripped her, cut her, photographed her, manipulated her limbs, nipped her flesh with the scalpel and finally, one of them, loaded the gun, thrust it in her hand and placed the nozzle on her head. This brought the performance to an end as other spectators finally intervened. This seminal artwork of Abramovic has invited many interpretations. Kristen Renzi brings out the contradictory aspects of this performance. She explains how the performance, on the one hand, was a moment of actual "intersubjective exchange" where the subjecthood of a body was finally recognized and the performance was stopped and "humanising interjection of performance art reverberated within the cold, impersonal space of the art museum." On the other hand, she poses a more disturbing question, "What if ... the performance was halted, not because Abramovic was seen as a life, but because she was viewed, and valued enough to save from destruction, as *art*?" ("Safety in Objects: Discourses of Violence and Value—The 'Rokeby Venus' and 'Rhythm 0,'" Renzi 2013, 124).

[4] For more details on Gina Pane's Tears of Blood ("Psyche" 1974), Ketty La Rocca's hands that speak ("Hands" 1975), Suzanne Santoro's photographs of withered female genitalia (*Towards New Expression* 1974), and Silvia Giambrone's stitching of an embroidered collar on her skin (*Teatro Anatomico* 2012), read Sam Johnson's article on female body, art and performance (2015).

[5] See https://www.kazoart.com/blog/en/orlan-a-feminist-icon-who-strived-for-social-change/ for more details on ORLAN's remaking her anatomy through "performance-operations," written by Max Hodge.

in an extreme close shot on the screen that is used by Ledgard to watch her. Ledgard is fascinated by the skin that he has himself manufactured. He ties up the victim, and attempts to tame and mold her as the obsessed stalker Ricky (Antonio Banderas) does in *Tie Me Up! Tie Me Down!* (1989). He then nurtures and replenishes the skin of the victim like the devoted lover Martin Benigno (Javier Camara) of *Talk to Her* (2002), and, like Benigno, is finally destroyed by that very skin. Vera, on the other hand, unable to reclaim her previous body, nevertheless attempts to reclaim some vestiges of her previous identity by returning to her old world. She constantly negotiates with her new skin, first by violating it and then by utilizing it. Her apparent subjugation toward the end of the film gives us an inkling of her final revolt. The skin plastered on her body as a penal inscription is reinterpreted by her as her only way of escape. The prison that her skin has become ultimately leads her to her path of freedom. Her skin becomes a site where subjection and resistance, fragility and resilience coalesce reminding us again of *Psycho* and the ironies inherent in a "repurposed" body. While Norman Bates decides to preserve Norma's dead skin, Norma scores a paradoxical victory by staying alive within Norman's live derma.

Masculine Female/Feminized Male: Resisting from the Margin

Body Horrors from *Psycho* to *The Skin I Live In* bring about the ambivalence of skin in relation to power. The skin may act as a medium of control by bearing the brunt of containment, as in the case of *Psycho* (where the taxidermized body of Norma Bates acts according to the dictates of her sick son), *The Silence of the Lambs* (where the skin of the victim and the extent of its suppleness determines her longevity), *Perfume* (where the skin is drained of its odor), and *The Skin I Live In* (where the skin lends an alien sexual identity to the wearer's body). However, that they may also be redefined and transformed from a means of subjugation to an effective weapon of retaliation is a statement that is unique in *The Skin I Live In*. It is the female skin of Vera/Vicente, nurtured and designed by the obsessed plastic surgeon, that turns against him. Unlike the victims of *Psycho* or *The Silence of the Lambs* or *Perfume*, Vera/Vicente could use the newly forged body to lull Ledgard into a false sense of security before killing him. He could somewhat reclaim his old life by returning to his mother and his love interest who is a lesbian. The final scene carries the hint of a sexually redefined body with the possibility of renegotiating with society at large.

All these films are preoccupied with simultaneous defiance and reinforcement of gender stereotypes. Fear of emasculation and/or the lure of it is explored through their treatment of the female body. The objectification of female bodies takes myriad forms in these films. For instance, Buffalo Bill and his real-life counterpart Ed Gein's stitching of a woman's skin suit to be donned by them, apart from being their attempts at erosion of their masculinity, are also acts of extreme savagery, which, again, they would like to think, are a male preserve. Their possession of a female body to be remodeled and preserved is not enough. They desire the female body to be a part of their very identity (like that of Norman in *Psycho*). Their bodies become spaces to be objectified and recreated that are in line with the body modification in vogue at present. Hence their masculinities (as well as their bodies) are layered unlike Robert Ledgard's (*The Skin I Live In*). Yet the narrative of the female body as a site of desire, objectification, and control runs through all of them. Robert's desire and control of the female body are based on three processes: the destruction of a natural body, its reconstruction into an idealized object, and its ruthlessly relentless preservation. But all these separate and yet overlapping strands of objectification and coveting of the female body (both as a source of identity and as a possessed property) cannot escape the conventional route of "male" fear, desire, and futile anger. The destruction of a female body is necessary, both in the fulfillment of various desires and in objectifying them. The purpose may be different but the process remains the same. A female body needs to be literally or figuratively flayed: to be worn or to be redesigned.

The Skin I Live In differs in that it has the opposite starting point but the same destination. The transformations that Vicente's body goes through are both a marker of a mad scientist's urge to dominate an unattainable body and a site of deformity, liminality, alterity, grotesqueness, and rebellion. Transgenesis and vaginoplasty may be seen here as sculptural mediums through medical invasion, which gives rise to several queries regarding the ambiguous status of Vera's body. Is she/he a masculine female or a feminized male? How can her/his body be classified as a sexual category? The camera that keeps Vera under constant surveillance records her struggles to both come to terms with, and yet resist, the sexuality imposed on his/her body. By shredding the skirts and frocks to pieces and by returning the cosmetics given to him/her, by slashing her breasts, throat, and abdomen with the sharp edges of a Cormac McCarthy book, Vera/Vicente continuously revolts against this process of forced gendering. Finally, it is Vicente's helpless succumbing to his invisibility, the gradual erasure of the parts of his body to be supplemented by completely different ones that petrify us: a body where death and life, man and woman, rebellion and surrender co-exist. This very surrender, the hopeless yielding of one's sexual identity, is used as a weapon in the end. Vicente, trapped in a body he cannot escape from, uses it as a mask (the skin that hides) to lull Robert into complacency before murdering him.

The Skin I Live In is one among many Almodóvar films where the filmmaker shows that projection of gender on screen strengthens the shared cultural definition of sexual identity. Films help manufacture the process of "gendering." And it is the body that becomes a space for the staging of that process. Bodies are sites where gender identities are created. Judith Butler in *Gender Trouble* defines the body as "a variable boundary, a surface whose permeability is politically regulated, a signifying practice within a cultural field of gender hierarchy and compulsory heterosexuality" (Butler 2012, 189). In the film, the gender hierarchy is well-established at the beginning. There are two sets of male adversaries: Robert and Zeca, and Robert and Vicente. In both these conflicts, the female body becomes a pawn. The body of Robert's wife becomes a trophy to be acquired/preserved by Zeca and Robert in the first half of the narrative. In the second half, it serves as a mask used by Vicente to win over Robert and then kill him. It is the female body that bears the brunt of this struggle for possession. It is burnt, revived, and then annihilated; it is again recreated, stitched, patched up, operated on, watched over, raped, imprisoned, and finally used as a weapon to kill. However, the sexually fluid bodies so frequent in Almodóvar films may also be read as his way of injecting confusion within the very notions of masculinity and femininity. For instance, this "gender hierarchy" is problematized in the sexual encounter of Vera/Vicente and Robert. The love-making of Robert and Vicente/Vera is a scene where the sexual identity and sexual orientation of both Vera and Robert are troubled. It is a scene where heterosexuality and homosexuality co-exist. The sexual intercourse between a male body and a female body, culled out of a male one, is an ironical dig at both "compulsory heterosexuality" and "gender hierarchy" as sexual identity is rendered transient and provisional. *The Skin I Live In* is thus one of the rare instances where body, identity, gender, and sexuality get so enmeshed that when Vera at the end utters the words: "I am Vicente," it becomes perfectly believable. Halberstam's idea of a fluid body is applicable to both Vera and Vicente and the entire aesthetics of physical transmutation: "Slowly but surely the outside becomes the inside and the hide no longer conceals or contains, it offers itself up as a text, as body, as monster" (1995, 7), and we may add, as a biological narrative that has liberated itself from the limiting bounds of sex and/or gender.

Conclusion

A cultural reading of marked and reforged skin in films like *Psycho*, *The Silence of the Lambs*, *Perfume*, and *The Skin I Live In* through the use of taxidermy, body modification, and body inscriptions bring forth the use of human and nonhuman anatomy as a canvas on which "the powerful" attempt to incise their marks of ownership. These films, along with numerous others, show how "the Others" are absorbed into the object world via their skin. Female skin, for instance, is equated to bird skin in *Psycho*. Norma's skin and birds' skin are the only raw materials of once-lived bodies that Norman uses to practice taxidermy. Again, female skin becomes a metaphoric and a literal raiment in *The Silence of the Lambs* while it becomes part of the geographical layout of Grasse in *Perfume*. *The Skin I Live In* adds another layer to this "skin fest." Robert Ledgard constructs a female skin by merging the human with the nonhuman (pig blood, for instance) via transgenesis thereby literally and corporeally tying up speciesism and sexism together. Here female skin is not transformed into something else. Rather, female skin is *created* to be mortared on a male body. Female skin is not only an object but a product of a cosmetic world created by a mad genius that gives a male body a new identity. Therefore, the role of skin in *Psycho*, *The Silence of the Lambs*, *Perfume*, and *The Skin I Live In* is to dislocate and render fluid the idea of a human body and to reinscribe itself as constitutive in the construction of sociocultural identities and its variances. While Norman's body assumes a contingent liminal sexual identity and Buffalo Bill at his own convenience slips in and out of his self-made female "hide," Vera's body is permanently both enmeshed with and distanced from its past anatomy. Her skin, besides being a corporeal biography of Gal written by Ledgard, is also a material autobiography of Vera who once was/still is Vicente.

Vera/Vicente's body, Buffalo Bill's hide, and Grenouille's skin, like so many other bodies that differ, have frequently been a staple of films. But stitching together the anguished corporeal experiences of the Others of Western patriarchy—the human female body, the sexually liminal body, and the animal body—with the thread of taxidermy began with two misfits at the margins of a highway, residing in a shared skin.

Bibliography

Adams, Carol J. 1994. *Neither Man nor Beast: Feminism and the Defense of Animals.* New York: Continuum.

Alberti, SJMM, ed. 2011. *The Afterlives of Animals: A Museum Menagerie.* London: University of Virginia Press.

Allen, Jeanne Thomas. 1985. "The Representation of Violence to Women: Hitchcock's Frenzy." *Film Quarterly* 38, no. 3 (Spring): 30–8. http://www.jstor.org/stable/1212541.

Atkinson, Michael, and Kevin Young. 2001. "Flesh Journeys: Neo Primitives and the Contemporary Rediscovery of Radical Body Modification." *Deviant Behavior* 22, no. 2: 117–46. doi: 10.1080/016396201750065018.

Bakhtin, Mikhail. 1984. *Rabelais and His World.* Translated by Helene Iswolsky. Bloomington: Indiana University Press.

Baldick, Chris, ed. 2001. *The Oxford Book of Gothic Tales.* Oxford: Oxford University Press.

Bann, Stephen. 1994. "Travelling to Collect: The Booty of John Bargrave and Charles Waterton." In *Travellers' Tales: Narratives of Home and Displacement*, edited by George Robertson, Melinda Mash, Lisa Tickner, Jon Bird, Barry Curtis and Tim Putnam, 155–63. London: Routledge.

Barker, Olivia. 2012. "'Playboy' Pays Nude Tribute to Marilyn Monroe." *USA Today.* Online. https://www.usatoday.com/story/life/people/2012/11/16/playboy-plays-tribute-to-nude-marilyn-monroe/1709637/.

Berger, John. 2009. *About Looking.* London: Bloomsbury Publishing.

Blackburn, Julia. 1991. *Charles Waterton: Traveller and Conservationist.* London: Century. https://archive.org/details/charleswaterton10000blac/page/n1/mode/2up. Accessed May 6, 2021.

Bloch, Robert. 2014. *Psycho.* London: Orion Publishing Group. Kindle.

Botting, Fred. 2008. *Limits of Horror: Technology, Bodies, Gothic.* Manchester: Manchester University Press.

Bozovic, Miran. 2004. "Of 'Farther Uses of the Dead to the Living': Hitchcock and Bentham." In *Hitchcock: Past and Future*, edited by Richard Allen and Sam Ishii Gonzales, 243–56. London: Routledge.

Bruhm, Steven. 1994. *Gothic Bodies: The Politics of Pain in Romantic Fiction*. Philadelphia: University of Pennsylvania Press.

Brush, Pippa. 1998. "Metaphors of Inscription: Discipline, Plasticity and the Rhetoric of Choice." *Feminist Review* 58, no. 1: 22–43. https://doi.org/10.1080/014177898339578.

Butler, Judith. 2012. *Gender Trouble: Feminism and the Subversion of Identity*. New York: Routledge.

Carson, Anne. "The Glass Essay." In *Glass, Irony and God*. New Directions Publishing Corporation, 1994. https://www.poetryfoundation.org/poems/48636/the-glass-essay.

Chandler, Charlotte. 2005. *It's Only a Movie: Alfred Hitchcock: A Personal Biography*. New York: Simon and Schuster.

Chion, Michel. 1999. *The Voice in Cinema*. Translated by Claudia Gorbman. New York: Columbia University Press.

Clover, Carol J. 1993. *Men Women and Chain Saws: Gender in the Modern Horror Film*. Princeton, NJ: Princeton University Press.

Cohen, Paula Marantz. 1995. *Alfred Hitchcock: The Legacy of Victorianism*. Kentucky: The University Press of Kentucky.

Colson, Rob. 2020. *Taxidermy Gone Wrong*. New York: HarperCollins.

Creaney, Conor. 2010. "Paralytic Animations: The Anthropomorphic Taxidermy of Walter Potter." *Victorian Studies* 53, no. 1: 7–35. Project Muse. doi:10.2979/victorianstudies.53.1.7. Accessed December 6, 2016.

Darwin, Charles. 1909. *The Origin of Species*. New York: P.F. Collier & Son.

Desmond, Jane. 2002. "Displaying Death, Animating Life: Changing Fictions of Liveness from Taxidermy to Animatronics." In *Representing Animals*, edited by Nigel Rothfels, 159–79. Bloomington: Indiana University Press.

Dickens, Charles. 2002. *Great Expectations*. London: Penguin Books.

Douchet, Jean. 2009. "Hitch and His Public." In *A Hitchcock Reader*, translated by Verena Andermatt Conley. Edited by Marshall Deutelbaum and Leland Poague. Wiley-Blackwell: Iowa State University Press.

Douglas, Mary. 2003. *Mary Douglas Collected Works, Volume II. Purity and Danger: An Analysis of the Concepts of Pollution and Taboo*. London: Routledge.

Durgnat, Raymond. 2002. *A Long Hard Look at Psycho*. London: British Film Institute.

Eastoe, Jane. 2012. *The Art of Taxidermy*. London: Pavilion Books. Kindle.

Edwards, Erin E. 2018. *The Modernist Corpse: Posthumanism and the Posthumous*. London: University of Minnesota Press.

Edwards Justin, D., and Rune Graulund. 2013. *Grotesque*. London: Routledge.

Elliott, Paul. 2011. *Hitchcock and the Cinema of Sensations: Embodied Film Theory and Cinematic Reception*. London: I.B. Tauris. Kindle.

Gottlieb, Sidney, ed. 1995. *Hitchcock on Hitchcock: Selected Writings and Interviews.* Berkeley: University of California Press.

Gregory, Helen, and Anthony Purdy. 2015. "Present Signs, Dead Things: Indexical Authenticity and Taxidermy's Nonabsent Animal." *Configurations* 23, no. 1: 62–92. doi:10.1353/con.2015.0004.

Greven, David. 2014. *Intimate Violence: Hitchcock, Sex, and Queer Theory.* New York: Oxford University Press.

Haeffner, Nicholas. 2005. *Alfred Hitchcock.* London: Pearson Longman.

Halberstam, Judith. 1995. *Skin Shows: Gothic Horror and the Technology of Monsters.* Durham, NC: Duke University Press.

Haraway, Donna. 1989. *Primate Visions: Gender, Race, and Nature in the World of Modern Science.* New York: Routledge.

Harvey, Sylvia. 1980. "Woman's Place: The Absent Family of Film Noir." In *Women in Film Noir*, edited by E. Ann Kaplan, 22–34. London: BFI Publishing.

Henning, Michelle. 2007. "Anthropomorphic Taxidermy and the Death of Nature: The Curious Art of Hermann Ploucquet, Walter Potter and Charles Waterton." *Victorian Literature and Culture* 35, no. 2: 663–78. http://www.jstor.org/stable/40347181. Accessed August 22, 2016.

Herman, David. *Narratology beyond the Human: Storytelling and Animal Life.* New York: Oxford University Press, 2018.

Hodge, Max. 2022. "ORLAN – A Feminist Icon Who Strived for Social Change." Online. https://www.kazoart.com/blog/en/orlan-a-feminist-icon-who-strived-for-social-change/. Accessed February 1, 2023.

Hornos, Maria Del Carmen Garrido. 2013. "Hitchcock and the Hollywood Production Code: Censorship and Critical Acceptance in the 1960s." In *Peeping through the Holes: Twenty-First Century Essays on Psycho*, edited by Eugenio M. Olivares Merino and Julio A. Olivares Merino, 1–24. Newcastle upon Tyne: Cambridge Scholars Publishing.

Hurley, Kelly. 1996. *The Gothic Body: Sexuality, Materialism, and Degeneration at the Fin de Siècle.* Cambridge, UK: Cambridge University Press.

Huxley, T.H. "On the Physical Basis of Life." In *Lay Sermons, Addresses, and Reviews*, 132–61. New York: Cambridge University Press, 2009.

Jacobs, Steven. 2013. *The Wrong House: The Architecture of Alfred Hitchcock.* Rotterdam: nai010 Publishers.

Johnson, Sam. 2015. "Five Radical Female Artists Who Used Their Body as a Canvas." Online. https://www.anothermag.com/art-photography/7942/five-radical-female-artists-who-used-their-body-as-a-canvas. Accessed March 2, 2020.

Kaplan, E. Ann. 1980. "Introduction." In *Women in Film Noir*, edited by E. Ann Kaplan, 1–5. London: BFI Publishing.

Koch, Gertrude. 1985. "Why Women Go to Men's Films." In *Feminist Aesthetics*, edited by Gisela Ecker. Translated by Harriet Anderson, 108–19. Boston: Beacon.

Kristeva, Julia. 1982. *Powers of Horror: An Essay on Abjection*. Translated by L.S. Roudiez. New York: Columbia University Press.

Lauretis, Teresa de. 1984. *Alice Doesn't: Feminism, Semiotics, Cinema*. Bloomington: Indiana University Press.

Marks, Laura U. 2000. *The Skin of the Film: Intercultural Cinema, Embodiment, and the Senses*. London: Duke University Press.

McGilligan, Patrick. 2003. *Alfred Hitchcock: A Life in Darkness and Light*. New York: HarperCollins.

Milgrom, Melissa. 2010. *Still Life: The Adventures of Taxidermy*. New York: Houghton Mifflin Harcourt. Kindle.

Modleski, Tania. 1982. "Never to Be Thirty-Six Years Old: *Rebecca* as Female Oedipal Drama." *Wide Angle* 5, no. 1: 34–41.

Modleski, Tania. 2005. *The Women Who Knew Too Much: Hitchcock and Feminist Theory*. New York: Routledge.

Monaco, James. 2009. *How to Read a Film: Movies, Media, and Beyond*. New York: Oxford University Press.

Mondal, Subarna. 2017. "Did He Smile His Work to See?"—Gothicism, Alfred Hitchcock's *Psycho* and the Art of taxidermy." *Palgrave Communications* 3: 17044. doi: 10.1057/palcomms.2017.44.

Mondal, Subarna. 2019a. "Dead but Not Gone: Female Body, Surveillance and Serial-Killing in Alfred Hitchcock's *Frenzy*." *Northern Lights* 17: 85–100. doi:10.1386/nl_00007_1.

Mondal, Subarna. 2019b. "One Grey Wall and One Grey Tower: The Bates World in Alfred Hitchcock's *Psycho*." In *Surveillance, Architecture and Control: Discourses on Spatial Culture*, edited by Susan Flynn and Antonia Mackay, 119–38. Cham: Palgrave Macmillan.

Mondal, Subarna. 2021. "Destruction, Reconstruction and Resistance: The Skin and the Protean Body in Pedro Almodóvar's Body Horror *The Skin I Live In*." Humanities 10, no. 1: 54. doi:10.3390/h10010054.

Moral, Tony Lee. 2013a. *Hitchcock and the Making of Marnie*. Maryland: Scarecrow Press.

Moral, Tony Lee. 2013b. *The Making of Hitchcock's The Birds*. Herts: Kamera Books.

Morris, Pat and Joanna Ebenstein. 2013. *Walter Potter's Curious World of Taxidermy*. London: Hachette.

Mulvey, Laura. 1975. "Visual Pleasure and Narrative Cinema." *Screen* 16, no. 3: 6–18.

Mulvey, Laura. 1990. "Afterthoughts on 'Visual Pleasure and Narrative Cinema' inspired by Duel in the Sun." In *Psychoanalysis and Cinema*, edited by E. Ann Kaplan, 24–35. London: Routledge.

Mulvey, Laura. 2006. *Death 24x a Second: Stillness and the Moving Image*. London: Reaktion Books.

Mulvey-Roberts, Marie. 2018. *Dangerous Bodies: Historicising the Gothic Corporeal*. Manchester: Manchester University Press.

Palmer, Joy. 2001. "Tracing Bodies: Gender, Genre, and Forensic Detective Fiction." *South Central Review* 18, no. 3/4: 54–71. doi: https://doi.org/10.2307/3190353.

Poliquin, Rachel. 2012. *The Breathless Zoo: Taxidermy and the Cultures of Longing*. University Park, Pennsylvania: Pennsylvania State University Press. Kindle.

Rebello, Stephen. 1990. *Alfred Hitchcock and the Making of Psycho*. New York: Integrated Media. Kindle.

Reich, Wilhelm. 1986. *The Sexual Revolution: Toward a Self-Governing Character Structure*. Translated by Therese Pol. New York: Farrar, Straus and Giroux.

Renzi, Kristen. 2013. "Safety in Objects: Discourses of Violence and Value—The 'Rokeby Venus' and 'Rhythm O.'" *SubStance* 42, no. 1: 120–45. http://www.jstor.org/stable/41818957.

Reyes, Xavier Aldana. 2014. *Body Gothic: Corporeal Transgression in Contemporary Literature and Horror Film*. Cardiff: University of Wales Press.

Ritvo, Harriet. 1987. *The Animal Estate: The English and Other Creatures in the Victorian Age*. Cambridge, MA: Harvard University Press.

Ritvo, Harriet. 1997. *The Platypus and the Mermaid, and Other Figments of the Classifying Imagination*. Harvard: Harvard University Press.

Rothman, William. 1982. *The Murderous Gaze*. Cambridge, MA: Harvard University Press.

Rothman, William. 2014. *Must We Kill the Thing We Love?: Emersonian Perfectionism and the Films of Alfred Hitchcock*. New York: Columbia University Press.

Schoell, William. 1985. *Stay Out of the Shower: Twenty-Five Years of Shocker Films Beginning with Psycho*. New York: Dembner.

Singer, Peter. 2015. *Animal Liberation*. London: The Bodley Head.

Skerry, Philip J. 2008. *Psycho in the Shower: The History of Cinema's Most Famous Scene*. New York: Continuum.

Smith, Joseph. 2009. *The Psycho File: A Comprehensive Guide to Hitchcock's Classic Shocker*. London: McFarland.

Spooner, Catherine. 2004. *Fashioning Gothic Bodies*. Manchester: Manchester University Press.

Spoto, Donald. 1999. *The Dark Side of Genius: The Life of Alfred Hitchcock*. New York: Da Capo Press.

Stefano, Joseph. 1959. "*Psycho* (1960) movie script – Screenplay for you." https://sfy.ru/?script=psycho. Online. Accessed February 16, 2017.

Stevenson, Robert Louis. 2011. *The Strange Case of Dr. Jekyll and Mr. Hyde and Other Tales*. Mumbai: Wilco Publishing House.

Stewart, Susan. 1993. *On Longing: Narratives of the Miniature, the Gigantic, the Souvenir, the Collection*. London: Duke University Press.

Stoker, Bram. 2000. *Dracula*. New York: Dover Publications.

Sullivan, Jack. 2006. *Hitchcock's Music*. London: Yale University Press.

Sumner, Don. 2010. *Horror Movie Freak*. China: Krauss Publications.

Toles, George. 2013. "'If Thine Eye Offend Thee … ': *Psycho* and the Art of Infection." In *Alfred Hitchcock: Centenary Essays*, edited by Richard Allen and S. Ishii Gonzales, 159–74. London: Palgrave Macmillan.

Truffaut, Francois, and Helen G. Scott. 1984. *Hitchcock: The Definitive Study of Alfred Hitchcock by Francois Truffaut*. New York: Simon and Schuster.

Turner, Bryan S. 2008. *The Body & Society: Explorations in Social Theory*. London: SAGE Publications Ltd. https://dx.doi.org/10.4135/9781446214329.

Waterton, Charles. 1891. *Wanderings in South America*. London, Paris and Melbourne: Cassell & Company. https://www.gutenberg.org/files/31811/31811-h/31811-h.htm.

Wells, H.G. 2005. *The Island of Dr. Moreau*. New York: Bantam Classic.

Wolfe, Cary. *Animal Rites: American Culture, the Discourse of Species, and Posthumanist Theory*. Chicago: The University of Chicago Press, 2003.

Wood, Robin. 2002. *Hitchcock's Films Revisited*. New York: Columbia University Press.

Zizek, Slavoj, ed. 1992. "In My Bold Gaze My Ruin Is Writ Large." *Everything You Always Wanted to Know about Lacan but Were Afraid to Ask Hitchcock*. London: Verso.

Videos cited

Asma, Stephen. "Taxidermy Monsters by Charles Waterton (1782–1865)." May 22, 2021. *Monsterology*, 10:09. Taxidermy monsters by Charles Waterton (1782–1865). YouTube. Accessed December 3, 2022.

Clark, Kate. "Human-Looking Faces on Animal Bodies: Taxidermy as Art | National Geographic." July 28, 2015. Interview taken by Katherine Carlson, 4:02. https://www.youtube.com/watch?v=JTYLPm-auj4.

Dubeau, Dylan and Andrew Strapp. "Jaguarundi: The Shadow of South America." May 28, 2022. Hosted by Danielle Dufault. *Animalogic*. 7:48. https://www.youtube.com/watch?v=WL1v9_lIr-M

The National Desk. "Taxidermied Kittens in Wedding Dresses? Just Another Day at the Morbid Anatomy Museum." September 22, 2016. *Morbid Anatomy Museum*, 1:53. Taxidermied Kittens in Wedding Dresses? Just Another Day at the Morbid Anatomy Museum. YouTube. Accessed December 3, 2022.

Natsuki. "The Startup Turning Human Ashes into Diamonds: Challengers by Freethink." 2022. 6:36. https://jp.voicetube.com/videos/172289

Peabody Museum: Archaeology and Ethnology. "FeeJee Mermaid." August 13, 2010, 2:04. https://www.youtube.com/watch?v=C1g7QbP4rM4

Films cited

Almodovar, Pedro, director. 1989. *Tie Me Up! Tie Me Down!* Miramax. 1 hr., 41 min. DVD.

Almodovar, Pedro, director. 2002. *Talk to Her*. Sony Pictures. 1 hr., 52 min. DVD.

Almodovar, Pedro, director. 2011. *The Skin I Live In*. Warner Bros. Pictures. 2 hr. DVD.

Bielinsky, Fabian, director 2005. *The Aura*. IFC Films. 2 hr., 14 min. Prime Video.

Demme, Jonathan, director. 1991. *The Silence of the Lambs*. Orion Pictures. 1 hr., 58 min. DVD.

Garrone, Matteo, director. 2002. *The Embalmer*. First Run, Four Ways. 1 hr., 40 min. DVD.

Guerrini, Mino, director. 1966. *Third Eye*. Arrow Video, Gothic Fantastico: Four Italian Tales of Terror. 1 hr., 38 min. Blu-ray.

Hitchcock, Alfred, director. 1927. *The Lodger: A Story of the London Fog*. Eros Films. 1 hr., 32 min. DVD.

Hitchcock, Alfred, director. 1929. *Blackmail*. Wardour Films. 1 hr., 25 min. DVD.

Hitchcock, Alfred, director. 1936. *Sabotage*. Gaumont-British Picture. 1 hr., 16 min. YouTube. https://www.youtube.com/watch?v=IbwC71cglyI

Hitchcock, Alfred, director. 1940. *Rebecca*. United Artists. 2 hr., 10 min. DVD.

Hitchcock, Alfred, director. 1943. *Shadow of a Doubt*. Universal Pictures. 1 hr., 48 min. DVD.

Hitchcock, Alfred, director. 1946. *Notorious*. RKO Pictures. 1 hr., 42 min. DVD.
Hitchcock, Alfred, director. 1948. *Rope*. Transatlantic Picture, 1 hr., 20 min. DVD.
Hitchcock, Alfred, director. 1949. *Under Capricorn*. Warner Bros. Pictures. 1 hr., 57 min. DVD.
Hitchcock, Alfred, director. 1951. *Strangers on a Train*. Warner Bros. Pictures. 1 hr., 41 min. DVD.
Hitchcock, Alfred, director. 1954. *Dial M for Murder*. Warner Bros. Pictures. 1 hr., 45 min. DVD.
Hitchcock, Alfred, director. 1954. *Rear Window*. Paramount Pictures. 1 hr., 52 min. DVD.
Hitchcock, Alfred, director. 1955. *To Catch a Thief*. Paramount Pictures. 1 hr., 46 min. DVD.
Hitchcock, Alfred, director. 1955. *The Trouble with Harry*. Paramount Pictures. 1 hr., 39 min. DVD.
Hitchcock, Alfred, director. 1956. *The Man Who Knew Too Much*. Paramount Pictures. 2 hr. DVD.
Hitchcock, Alfred, director. 1956. *The Wrong Man*. Warner Bros Pictures. 1 hr., 45 min. DVD.
Hitchcock, Alfred, director. 1958. *Vertigo*. Paramount Pictures. 2 hr., 8 min. DVD.
Hitchcock, Alfred, director. 1959. *North by North West*. Metro-Goldwyn-Mayer. 2 hr., 16 min. DVD.
Hitchcock, Alfred, director. 1960. *Psycho*. Paramount Pictures. 1 hr., 49 min. DVD.
Hitchcock, Alfred, director. 1963. *The Birds*. Universal Pictures. 1 hr., 59 min. DVD.
Hitchcock, Alfred, director. 1964. *Marnie*. Universal Pictures. 2 hr., 10 min. DVD.
Hitchcock, Alfred, director. 1972. *Frenzy*. Universal Pictures. 1 hr., 56 min. DVD.
Hooper, Tobe, director. 1974. *The Texas Chainsaw Massacre*. Bryanston Pictures. 1 hr., 23 min. 1974. DVD.
Larraz, Jose Rammon, director. 1971. *Deviation*. VHS. 1 hr., 29 min. DVD.
Pálfi, György, director. 2006. *Taxidermia*. Regent Releasing. 1 hr., 31 min. DVD.
Rhys, Theo, director. 2021. *Stuffed*. 19 min. https://www.youtube.com/watch?v=Rlkcol3hg0U. YouTube.
Rourke, Austin, director. 2020. *A Strange Calm*. AFI Conservatory. 13 min. https://www.youtube.com/watch?v=yggHy5dHM68
Rowe, Aaron, director. 2020. *Bondo*. DeathRowe Productions. 16 min. https://www.imdb.com/title/tt13384978/.
Silverman, Kaja. 1996. *The Threshold of the Visible World*. New York: Manchester United Press.

Six, Tom, director. 2009. *The Human Centipede* (First Sequence). IFC Films. 1 hr., 32 min. DVD.
Trier, Lars von, director. 2018. *The House That Jack Built*. Scream Factory. 2 hr., 32 min. Blu-ray.
Tykwer, Tom, director. 2006. *Perfume: The Story of a Murderer*. DreamWorks Pictures. 2 hr., 27 min. DVD.
Williams, Bert, director. 1965. *The Nest of the Cuckoo Birds*. Bert Williams Motion Pictures. 1 hr., 21 min. DVD.

Index

abhumans 9–12, 20, 37
abject, abjection 19, 26, 27, 88
Abramovic, Marina 137
acousmatic 42
active-passive binary 5, 22, 120–2
Akeley, Carl Ethan 53–5
Akeley, Mary Jobe's *The Wilderness Lives Again* 54
ambivalence 28, 97, 107, 108, 119, 120, 138
American Museum of Natural History 52, 53
Andrews, Roy Chapman 53
Animal Liberation Movement 21, 40
animal studies 8, 21, 22
animal/human 11, 25, 39, 124, 132
anthropocentrism, anthropocentric 19, 20, 21, 101
anthropomorphism, anthropomorphic 7, 9–12, 19, 20, 31, 46, 47, 52, 60
assemblage 33, 77
attic, attic attack 75–8, 83
autoiconization 9
avian, avian imagery 8, 72, 78

basement 6, 12, 23, 24, 26, 35, 50, 51, 57, 78, 89, 124, 133
Bass, Saul 2, 86, 87
Bentham, Jeremy 9
Bill, Buffalo 12, 123–5, 133, 139, 142
biocentric 21
bisexuality: female, male 120, 121, 129
Body Gothic and Corporeal Gothic 3, 5, 11, 14, 15, 71
Body Horror/s 2, 6, 12, 13, 15–18, 58, 71, 123, 125, 138
body modification/s 39, 133, 134, 139, 141
Bourgeois, Louise 128, 136
British Museum 46, 106
Bullock, William 71

cinema spectatorship 13
Cock Robin, The Death and Burial of 20, 29, 31, 32
consent theory 26, 27
corpse power 104, 113
cosmetology 126, 127, 133
curiosity cabinet/s 16, 31, 41, 42, 43, 47, 59

death care company/ companies 63
defilement 112, 113
detective novels, detective films 113, 114, 116, 117
diorama 16, 40, 50–3, 55, 61, 62
dismemberment 15, 96, 110, 115
docile 17, 32, 118
dollhouse 49, 50, 51, 52

embodied spectatorship 5, 44
exploitation film 13, 17, 82, 100

feline 20, 24, 26–8, 81
female spectatorship 120, 121
female subjectivity 18
feminist psychoanalytic 4, 119
femme fatale 98, 127
fetishism, fetishist, fetishistic 8, 103, 123
Field Museum of Chicago 53
Fiji Mermaid 61
filth 103, 107, 112
Fishwick, Jack 59
forensic 105, 106, 113, 114, 117˚
Freud, Sigmund 5, 120

gaze 5, 94, 102, 103, 105, 117, 118, 120
Gein, Ed 3, 58, 139

habitat diorama 52, 53, 59
Hagen's Body Worlds 133
Hays Code 2, 96
Hefner, Hugh 99
Herman, David 21

Hermann, Bernard 2, 87
humanimals 10, 12
hummingbirds 71

installation/s 8, 11, 16, 20, 24

Kelly, Grace 73, 74, 78, 119, 121

Levi-Strauss 108
liminal, liminality 10, 14, 20, 24, 29, 37, 38, 40, 95, 96, 132, 139, 142
Liverpool Museum 71

macabre 29, 34, 42, 57, 58, 59, 60
madhouse cue 87
mad surgeon, surgeon 131, 138
mainstream: narrative cinema, Hollywood films/cinema 2, 4, 18, 56, 68, 72, 96, 119, 126
male spectator 5
masculinity 120, 122, 134, 139, 140
matricide 51, 104
Mayer, Emily 7, 95, 96
    Last Resting Place (Their Death in My Hands) 95
miniature 26, 28, 29, 48–52, 58
misogyny 118, 119
Miss Havisham 22, 23, 26–8
Monroe, Marilyn 99
monster/s 12–14, 16, 38–40, 92, 124, 125, 132, 133, 141
montage 76, 88, 91
Morgan, Polly 7, 45
mount 25, 27, 37, 46, 53, 56, 92, 110
mourning technology 63
multispecies 19, 24
museum 16, 24, 28, 33, 46, 50, 53, 137

"Nanoq—Flat Out and Bluesome" 59
noir films 97–9, 107, 127

objectification, objectify, objectified 117, 120, 136, 139
Other 5, 14, 15, 20, 29, 37, 92

Paramount 2, 96, 97
patriarchy 72, 84, 98, 110, 112, 119, 121, 122, 142

plastic surgeries, plastic surgeon 133, 134, 138
Playboy 99
Ploucquet, Hermann 10, 16, 46, 52, 58–60
police procedural 15, 17, 105, 106
pollutant 108, 113
postwar, postwar America 97–9
Potter, Walter 10, 16, 27–9, 31, 49, 50, 52, 58–60
    "The Kittens' Wedding" 20, 24, 26–9
primatology 21

Rousseau, Henri: *The Snake Charmer* 135

scopophilia 5, 102
Second Wave Feminism 97
serial-killing, serial killer 15, 19, 33, 37, 105, 106, 107, 113
sexism 19, 21, 22, 24, 32, 40, 103, 113, 117, 141
shower scene, shower murder 3, 17, 76, 77, 85, 88–91, 93–6, 100, 102–4
slasher/s 3, 6, 13, 17, 58, 100–3, 106, 116, 127
Sloane, Hans 46
speciesism 19–22, 24, 32, 40, 113, 141
spectatorship 5, 13, 44, 120, 121
stuffed 8, 19, 21, 22, 28, 36, 70–3, 85, 97, 129
surgery: cosmetic, plastic 126, 133, 134
surgical horror 13, 14, 16, 131, 133, 134
surveillance 106, 113, 116–18, 130, 140

tableau/s 19, 20, 26–9, 31, 46, 48–51, 60, 62
taxidermy
    contemporary 7, 18, 45, 59
    "crap" 60
    eighteenth-century 45, 46
    ethical 7, 55
    fin de siècle 52, 53
    re-creation (in taxidermy) 15, 33–5, 46, 56, 61, 74, 92
    Rogue taxidermist 59, 60
    Schwendeman's Taxidermy Studio 58, 59

sixteenth- and seventeenth-century taxidermy 41–3, 46, 47
thing culture 9, 16, 19
twentieth-century 52, 55, 56
Titian's *Venus of Urbino* 135
Titian's *Venus with an Organist and Cupid* 135
transgenesis 129, 132, 139, 141
trophy 7, 19, 140

uncanny 5, 30, 31, 110

vaginoplasty 129, 139
Victorian bride/s 20, 24, 26–9

Villalta, Guillermo Perez: *Dionysus Finds Ariadne in Naxos* 135
vivisection 10, 11, 38
voyeurism 4, 105, 106, 116, 117, 121

Walker, Ken Roy 59
Walton Hall 33, 36, 39, 48, 52
Waterton, Charles 10, 16, 33, 34, 36–40, 48, 49, 52, 58, 59
  John Bull and the National Debt 38, 39
  Martin Luther after His Fall 38
  Nondescript 20, 33, 34, 37–40

www.ingramcontent.com/pod-product-compliance
Lightning Source LLC
Chambersburg PA
CBHW052050300426
44117CB00012B/2052